WOMEN MURD
BY THE MEN THE
Constance A. Bean, ᴍ.ᴘ.ʜ.

SOME ADVANCE REVIEWS

"The most compelling, original, and comprehensive presentation of this crucial topic I've ever encountered. The women's stories presented in detail in this book are very frightening; they could be stories about our mothers, sisters, or even ourselves. Yet the book is enlightening, preventive medicine. Every woman needs to read this book and read it right now!"

Martha Loss
Corporate Health and Management Consultant
Newton, Massachusetts

"In clear and compelling language, buttressed by unbelievable but documented examples, Constance Bean pinpoints specific danger signs for women. . . . The very women who think they may be least in need of the information in this book may well be those in the most danger. . . . A copy of this book should be in the hands of every law enforcement official in this country. Wide dissemination of this book holds the promise of actually saving lives, not only of the potential victim herself, but of her children who silently bear witness to daily nightmares within their own homes."

Barbara F. Graham
Writer and Editor
Weston, Massachusetts

"Provides a valuable service in the frank discussion of victims of abuse and their abusers . . . Could possibly serve to save the lives of women who are at risk but are unaware of the risk factors involved. . . ."

Sabine Haberland Cray
Editor, *Mount Holyoke Alumnae Quarterly*
Mount Holyoke College

"An essential and insightful addition to the body of evidence growing in the field of domestic violence. . . . Bean's work proves invaluable as it moves away from blaming the victim by focusing on the individual obstacles and challenges faced by women involved with violent men. . . . A must read for all professionals struggling to liberate women from the clutches of abusive partners."

Jean C. Haertl
Director, Victim Advocacy Program
Framingham Police Women's Protective Services
Massachusetts

NOTES FOR PROFESSIONAL LIBRARIANS AND LIBRARY USERS

This is an original book title published by Harrington Park Press, an imprint of The Haworth Press, Inc. Unless otherwise noted in specific chapters with attribution, materials in this book have not been previously published elsewhere in any format or language.

CONSERVATION AND PRESERVATION NOTES

The paper used in this publication meets the minimum requirements of American National Standard for Information Sciences — Permanence of Paper for Printed Material, ANSI Z39.48-1984.

Women Murdered by the Men They Loved

HAWORTH Women's Studies
Ellen Cole, PhD and Esther Rothblum, PhD
Senior Co-Editors

New, Recent, and Forthcoming Titles:

When Husbands Come Out of the Closet by Jean Schaar Gochros

Prisoners of Ritual: An Odyssey into Female Genital Circumcision in Africa by Hanny Lightfoot-Klein

Foundations for a Feminist Restructuring of the Academic Disciplines edited by Michele Paludi and Gertrude A. Steuernagel

Hippocrates' Handmaidens: Women Married to Physicians by Esther Nitzberg

Waiting: A Diary of Loss and Hope in Pregnancy by Ellen Judith Reich

God's Country: A Case Against Theocracy by Sandy Rapp

Women and Aging: Celebrating Ourselves by Ruth Raymond Thone

A Woman's Odyssey into Africa: Tracks Across a Life by Hanny Lightfoot-Klein

Women's Conflicts About Eating and Sexuality: The Relationship Between Food and Sex by Rosalyn M. Meadow and Lillie Weiss

Anorexia Nervosa and Recovery: A Hunger for Meaning by Karen Way

Women Murdered by the Men They Loved by Constance A. Bean

Reproductive Hazards in the Workplace: Mending Jobs, Managing Pregnancies by Regina Kenen

Our Choices: Women's Personal Decisions About Abortion by Sumi Hoshiko

Women Murdered by the Men They Loved

Constance A. Bean, MPH

Harrington Park Press
An Imprint of The Haworth Press, Inc.
New York • London • Norwood (Australia)

ISBN 1-56023-003-7

Published by

Harrington Park Press, an imprint of The Haworth Press, Inc., 10 Alice Street, Binghamton, NY 13904-1580

Library of Congress Cataloging-in-Publication Data

Bean, Constance A.
    Women murdered by the men they loved / Constance A. Bean.
        p.   cm.
    Includes bibliographical references and index.
    ISBN 1-56023-003-7 (acid-free paper)
    1. Murder—United States—Case studies. 2. Women—United States—Crimes against—Case studies. 3. Uxoricide—United States—Case Studies. 4. Crimes of passion—United States—Case studies. I. Title.
HV6529.B43 1992b
364.1'523'0973—dc20   91-23624
                                                                            CIP

CONTENTS

ABOUT THE AUTHOR

Constance A. Bean, MPH, has spent fourteen years as Coordinator of Health Education at the Massachusetts Institute of Technology. Formerly she spent five years as Lecturer in Health Sciences at Northeastern University. A co-founder of the Boston Association for Childbirth Education, Inc., she is also the author of several books including *Methods of Childbirth*, (Doubleday, 1972), *Labor and Delivery, An Observer's Diary,* (Doubleday, 1977), *Methods of Childbirth Revised: A Completely New Book* (Doubleday, 1982), *The Better Back Book* (Morrow, 1989), and *Methods of Childbirth: A Completely Updated Version of a Classic Work for Today's Woman* (Morrow, 1990). A member of the American College Health Association, Health Education Section and the International Childbirth Education Association, she earned her BA from Mount Holyoke College and her MPH degree from Yale University. She is currently spending a year lecturing, writing, and consulting in health education.

Chapter One

"Who Done It? It Was the Husband"

Why do men kill their wives and lovers? And their ex-wives? Who are the men who murder, and are others at risk from these dangerous men as well? Did anyone — the dead woman, her family, or her friends — have any premonition of her fate? In particular, why have so many — for so long — been unaware of how often women are killed, not by strangers on the street but by their mates?

"Woman shot by estranged husband" is not an uncommon heading for a short article on the inside pages of any newspaper. "Woman stabbed by boyfriend" usually elicits no more than a simple announcement of the event (if that) or of the man's subsequent scheduled court appearance. A motive is rarely presented, with the possible exceptions of alleged "jealousy" of another man or "rage." Most readers turn to the rest of the day's news with little knowledge of the significance of this information or any way of understanding what it has to do with their lives.

Also rarely presented is the frequency with which women are murdered by the men with whom they live. Statistically, a woman is in far more danger in her own bedroom than on the seediest of urban streets at four o'clock in the morning! At risk are rich and famous women as well as poor and disadvantaged ones. At least one-third, and probably one-half, of female homicide victims are "done in" by their husbands or lovers. Yet, despite its prevalence, this crime is only beginning to be recognized and adequately punished.

Amidst family and friends, a man and a woman walk down the aisle and make promises to each other that often include the words "until death do us part." Their prior relationship may have been long or short, but what lies ahead is largely unknown. Indeed, at

1

least one out of three, if not half, of those who marry will part at some point. They will become "not together now." Relationships and marriages may dissolve in disappointed hopes. The parting may occur not because of a decision to walk separate paths but because the man murders the woman. "I could kill you" becomes fact. The two are indeed parted by death.

If the murder case has drama and intrigue it rivets, temporarily, public attention. However, the murder is seldom placed in the context of a regularly occurring event. Every day, women are beaten to death, strangled, slashed, shot, or sent over a cliff by their mates. We learn about only a few. Some will be described in these pages.

A European man with aristocratic connections meets and marries an American heiress. Years later, Claus Von Bulow (see Chapter Six) is accused of attempting to kill his blonde socialite wife at least twice in her Newport mansion by injecting her with insulin.

A man in Texas, posing as a psychologist, meets a beautiful and vivacious girl with loving parents. Patricia is a hometown cheerleader who has no reason to distrust anyone. Her new husband takes out an insurance policy on her life. Just days after their wedding, while the couple is still honeymooning in New Orleans, a staged hit-and-run accident takes her life. The crime leaves Patricia's New Jersey parents forever bereft of their only child. The details are known only because Dillman (1988) wrote a book about the case.

A military physician, Jeffrey MacDonald, was convicted of killing his pregnant wife and two small daughters in a brutal club and knife slaying (described in Chapter Six). The fact that the husband was a physician played heavily in the news coverage of this case. If not for his father-in-law's dogged pursuit of justice, the killer would never have been identified, and the case would have disappeared quickly from the news.

Steven Steinberg, an Arizona salesman and restaurateur, claimed bushy-haired intruders were the perpetrators of the dastardly deed. The stylish, silver and white master bedroom became blood-soaked beyond belief during Elana's futile struggle to save her life. This case (described in Chapter Six) remained in the news for a time only because the event occurred in what was seen as an unlikely suburban setting. This raised it from the usual category of "domestic violence."

Robert Marshall, an apparently successful New Jersey business-man and father of three sons, took his attractive blonde wife of more than twenty years out for dinner one evening. On the way home from Atlantic City he pulled his car off the highway into a wooded picnic area where his wife was shot by hired killers (see Chapter Six). The orphaned sons and the wide number of people who knew the Marshalls in their community were factors that wid-ened the story beyond the usual news coverage.

Among Charles Stuart's possessions was a book describing the Marshall case. Three months before Stuart's fatal leap off a Boston bridge, after a hospital birthing class, Charles drove to the Mission Hill section of Boston where his pregnant wife, Carol, was shot to death (see Chapter Six). Charles blamed the shootings on a black man in a hooded sweatshirt, thereby stirring racial tensions. The case evoked wide publicity because of the circumstances surround-ing this death, not because another woman was murdered. Much of the news coverage occurred before the husband became the suspect. After his dramatic leap, intrigue flared anew because so much mys-tery still remained. No one could understand exactly what really happened that night or why. Could he really have killed her for the insurance money? Perhaps, unknowingly, other women were also at risk from their mates.

A man is barred by a court restraining order from entering his home after repeated violent assaults on his wife. This becomes a brief news item only because he is running for state office.

If the method of death is sufficiently bizarre, its news value is enhanced. In another case (*The New York Times*, Sept. 19, 1990) a New York restaurant worker was accused of murdering his girlfriend, boiling her dismembered body, and feeding it to his cat. Monika Beerle, a dance student from Switzerland, was killed when she tried to throw Daniel Rakowitz out of her apartment where he had been living for two months. He beat her, stabbed her, and cut her up. The court found him innocent of intentional murder by rea-son of insanity. It was noted that he could be released after spending as little as six months in the mental institution.

In 1986, Richard Crafts, a commercial airline pilot and part-time local police officer, was convicted of murdering his wife and disposing of her body by putting it through a wood chipper one snowy November night (see Chapter Six).

A news story (*Boston Globe*, Oct. 3, 1990) described a woman's body as having been "jettisoned" into the back seat of the family car after her 41-year-old husband had allegedly strangled her. Before he was charged with the killing he sobbingly claimed to reporters that she was "my best friend." Cheryl's body was found in the parking lot of the popular Emerald Mall in Attleborough, Massachusetts.

One missing persons case, still open, is that of Virginia Douglas who was traveling to Maine with her husband Frank of 46 years. Her husband says that Virginia left their car to go to a mall restroom and never returned. Her pocketbook was found in the car. An extensive and widely publicized three year search has failed to solve this mystery. She has not been seen since. Her husband is not accused of anything.

At the time of Virginia's disappearance Frank Douglas told police that on the evening before the impromptu trip, he and his wife had had an argument after he mistakenly locked her out of their home. He further volunteered that his wife had mood swings and was sometimes depressed. His two daughters are of the opinion that he killed their mother. The Lexington police chief considers the husband, still living in the family home, as a suspect (*Boston Globe*, Sept. 1, 1991).

A woman gives her boyfriend the money for the down payment on their condominium. Shortly thereafter she disappears from sight. Friends suspect that her body may be at the bottom of Boston Harbor because she went out with her self-serving boyfriend on his boat. These friends had felt uncomfortable about this relationship. She is one of countless women who simply disappear. Her story was never reported. She is "missing" and her mother in Germany has not pursued the case.

IS IT SERIOUS? IS HELP ON THE WAY?

Women, knowing the danger and fearing for their lives, unsuccessfully seek the protection of the police and legal system. However, these women may die because no crime has yet been committed.

Pam Guenther, living near Denver, was shot to death in a parking lot (*The New York Times*, Apr. 21, 1989). Just a week before the murder, her former husband, Dave, held her hostage at home for six hours before the police talked him into letting her go. She escaped to a shelter, safe for the moment, but he wanted her dead.

In Cambridge, Massachusetts, a pregnant woman unsuccessfully sought police protection. Her husband had committed no crime. There was only the threat. Shortly thereafter Pamela Dunn's body was discovered in a Cambridge dumpster (*Boston Globe*, May 12, 1987).

Husbands accused of murdering their wives almost never have a criminal record or a known psychiatric history (U.S. Department of Justice Report, 1986). Most often, they appear to have no more problems than might occur in many households. In fact, bail has been low and sentences often light just because the accused, even when convicted, is not seen as a threat to society. He is dangerous only to his wife.

The common perception is that these murders are rare, and that the incidents are "anecdotal." They are commonly seen as an aberration that has little to do with everyday marriage and love relationships. Whatever the ascribed motive, if any, the killings are seldom described as either a widespread societal problem requiring answers and solutions or one with possible warning signs for women. (National Woman Abuse Prevention Project, Fact Sheet, 1990. See Resource list on Understanding Domestic Violence.)

Men attack wives or female partners with alarming regularity (Bureau of Justice Statistical Special Report, Aug., 1986). The intent is to injure, maim, and murder. A man may single-mindedly hunt a woman down (while proclaiming his undying love) to injure or kill her. Sometimes a man will track an ex-wife or lover for years for the sole purpose of killing her (Walker, 1989). For this reason, some women have even sought to change names and identities.

A man imprisoned for attempted murder of his girlfriend was released on parole from a six-year sentence without the knowledge of either the woman or her family. The very day of his release he stopped by her workplace, ordered her into his car, and, a few miles down the highway, killed her with a knife.

The cases described above are by no means bizarre and isolated incidents. In Massachusetts, a woman is killed by her husband or lover every nine days. In the United States, at least four women are murdered by their partners every day (National Coalition Against Domestic Violence, 1988). Walker (1989) gives the following statistics: During the first two months of 1987, seven women were murdered by abusive mates in the metropolitan Denver area. By the end of the year, the number was 19. A Norfolk, Virginia women's shelter counted 69 dead battered women within the first nine months of 1987. American homicide statistics compiled by the Centers for Disease Control in Atlanta, Georgia, were analyzed by psychologist Angela Browne and sociologist Kirk Williams. They found an increase in the number of women being killed by abusive partners in 35 states; in 25 states, most of these women were killed after they separated from or divorced their male partners (Browne and Williams, 1989). Sociologist Murray Straus estimates that, in any society, between 25 and 67% of all homicides occur within the family and inside the home (Straus, Gelles, and Steinmetz, 1980).

Violence has many faces. There is violence in the streets, murder by stranger, serial murder, child abduction and murder, and child abuse from which children lose their lives. Women are battered in their homes, with perhaps only one in ten of such cases reported. However, how many people realize the life-and-death reality of the alarming statistics about women murdered by men they loved?

Chapter Two

The Root of the Problem

When a murder occurs, the search is for motive as well as weapon. Hypotheses generally center around passion, greed, and uncontrollable anger. All of the above related factors have often been seen as at least somewhat comprehensible, if deplorable. After all, say some, how can a man stomach his wife's affair with another man or her consideration of another relationship? Although money as a reason for murder is perceived as unacceptable knavery, acquisition of financial resources is recognized as a goal toward which, of necessity, most strive throughout much of their lives. Regarding uncontrollable rage, anger is an emotion with which everyone must struggle, and all deal with it imperfectly. "A man can take just so much" has been one way the killer's apologist has attempted to explain an apparently senseless murder.

Given the high rate of women murdered, are the above reasons sufficient to explain why so many women are murdered by their mates? Indeed, the factors of passion, greed, and rage in any combination are powerful, even as they conflict with values and behaviors adjudged acceptable.

Murder is the ultimate act of obliterating the rights of another. It is against the law, although many states recognize exceptions under certain circumstances, and wife murder has often been judged less harshly than murder by stranger. Violence against children has often been associated and confused with child discipline.

Marriage is purportedly a loving relationship entered into freely by both parties. Can love and murder somehow go hand in hand? If the loving relationship sours, why do some men hang on so tightly to the relationship that these men will try to kill their partners if they leave or even attempt to leave?

"THERE HAS TO BE MORE"

The immediate motive for killing Elana Steinberg (see Chapter Six), appeared to be Steve's free-wheeling lifestyle and disintegrating financial situation. Steve needed money and he did not want questions from his wife. He said his wife "drove him to it" by her spending.

In Richard Crafts' ingenious "woodchipper" plot (see Chapter Six), the immediate cause of the crime is considered, by those who knew the couple, to be his wife's divorce threat. She had backed away from divorce a number of times in the past, but in that fall of 1986 she appeared serious. This could cost him money and force him to make unwelcome changes in his life.

Dr. Jeffrey MacDonald, it is conjectured, may have gone on his bloody rampage (see Chapter Six) because he felt his authority challenged by his wife's proffered information from her psychology class (see Chapter Six). He saw himself, and certainly not his wife Colette, as the expert. Enraged, he used a club, knives, and an ice pick to murder his wife and daughters.

Margaret's husband threatened her with death repeatedly for twenty years. Frequently, for no discernible reason, he placed a gun to her head. Anything or everything might produce his rage, especially her desire to leave him. There was obviously no other man involved in Margaret's life. Her story is not uncommon. Five times Margaret made her escape only to be hunted down. All legal restraining orders proved useless. When Margaret finally managed to hide, and could not be flushed out, her beloved nineteen-year-old daughter Elizabeth became his victim. She was shot through a pillow while she slept in her bed. His reason? He said his wife would not come home. Neither mother nor daughter had considered that Elizabeth could be in danger. The two, in constant contact, had spoken by telephone just three hours before Elizabeth was murdered. There was no doubt about his intent to kill, or why. On tape, he stated his plan before the crime, declaring that now his wife "will be punished for the rest of her life."

Claus Von Bulow's apparent motive was money, or rather, more money (see Chapter Six). There was an additional reason he may have considered murder. His mistress (Alexandra) wanted marriage. Von Bulow could not have divorced his wife Sunny to marry Alexandra without losing his inheritance of at least fifteen million dollars. The trust income from his wife Sunny was nothing compared with the bigger prize awaiting only her death. The guilty verdict was overturned at Von Bulow's second trial.

Why did Charles Stuart apparently want his pregnant wife, Carol, to die? After Charles's fatal leap from the bridge appeared to confirm his guilt, evidence accumulated about his possible motive. The key seemed to be the life insurance which was divided among several companies. During the weeks and months before her death, Charles had taken out several life insurance policies on Carol. Charles told friends (see Chapter Six) that he needed capital to open a restaurant. He had expensive tastes as well as big dreams which a stay-at-home wife would thwart or delay. From all appearances, Charles schemed to trade his wife and soon-to-be-born son for a restaurant.

When examining cases where men have murdered their female partners and for which there is available background information, the assumed motive seems inadequate to explain the enormity of the crime. Greed, lust, and rage are powerful motives, but many men with these emotions do not murder their wives. Those who do kill often profess love for their wives. Some even kill themselves after murdering their female partners. What is going on? These stories are the tip of the iceberg: There has to be more.

TODAY'S WOMAN

The role of women, in both the family and society, plays a large part in placing women at risk for murder. Women are slowly becoming less economically dependent on men, giving them more choices. Progress continues in the improvement of women's status and women's rights (including property, political, and legal) as well as employment opportunities. Women also have more input into their health care choices although problems remain in all of the above.

Women still earn less, have lower pensions, and often pay into the Social Security system without deriving any benefit. They may receive lower benefits because of their work patterns or employment status. Many work very hard at vital tasks and yet are not considered "gainfully" employed. Large numbers remain economically dependent on the men in their lives, thereby increasing their vulnerability to all forms of male control. No-fault divorce, without the former possibility of generous alimony, has not been an unmitigated boon for women. During the first year after divorce the standard of living for women and children drops an average of 73%, while men's rises 42% (National Woman Abuse Prevention Project, Fact Sheet, 1990).

In the home, the trend is toward shared parenting and shared responsibility for household tasks, although studies show that practice does not approach equality. There are wide variations in today's households—choices made, the roles and responsibilities of each, and the ways power and money are shared. However, many women as well as men continue to adhere to traditional roles. They state that they would have it no other way, even as they recognize inherent inequalities and the possible effects of man's job loss (or divorce). These women may, in fact, not be disempowered. They may prefer to remain the major nurturers and care-givers of their own and extended families, to not give away these functions. Other women who appear to have a more equal marriage may be very much disempowered, and at considerable risk for violence, with very little power to set appropriate limits and standards for behavior within the home.

By the mid-1970s, the topic of physical and emotional violence against women surfaced, including assault and battery in the home. Other problems reflecting women's vulnerability to attack such as acquaintance rape, incest, and other violence issues came out of the shadows into public awareness. Women's shelters were organized by women as temporary havens for women and their children. These shelters acknowledge, with bricks and mortar, that assault and battery in the home—man against woman—is more than a rare, isolated incident. The legal system has only begun to respond.

Public sensitivity about demeaning sexist comments and behaviors has increased, even as those events continue to occur. And violent behavior against women may still be blamed on women, because they are seen as too submissive, too provocative, or too "liberated." What many fail to recognize is that the existing inequities with regard to women may affect safety levels of women, not on the streets, but in their homes.

This book is about murder. Murder requires the acknowledgement of its significance for all, and is no longer to be viewed as rare. Whatever progress has been made outside the home, whatever success the woman may have achieved in her profession, within the home she is as much at risk as ever.

THE CLUES: "BACK TO THE BEGINNING" IN AMERICA AND BEFORE . . .

The problem is neither a new issue nor a reflection of today's world. It goes far back into history. When trying to understand why wife and female partner murder exists in today's society, some factors can be identified by examining women's lives at the time United States history began.

Woman murder did not start then, and it is by no means exclusive to the United States. There are many cultures in which women have fared far worse and continue to live in almost complete subjugation and servitude. The beliefs, attitudes, and practices that hold the potential for violence against women are found worldwide and are evident throughout recorded human history.

Thousands of executions of so-called witches took place in Europe during the late fifteenth and early sixteenth centuries. Eighty-five percent of those killed were women (Ehrenreich and English, 1989). Some writers place the number of deaths far higher. The method of killing was usually live burning at the stake. It occurred in Germany, Italy, France and England; 900 "witches" were destroyed in a single year in the Wurzburg, Germany area. The reasons are described by Ehrenreich and English and others as misogynist fantasies such as rendering men impotent, devouring babies, or poisoning livestock. Many of the "crimes" involved providing contraceptive measures, performing abortions, and offering drugs to ease labor pain. Some of the healing methods these women used to treat men, women, and children meet the test of modern times. In the New World of the American colonies, plants and herbs known to the Native Americans were added to female lore (Ehrenreich and English, 1989; Lyons and Petrucelli, 1987).

Healing itself could be seen as a "crime." While women were developing knowledge of bones and muscles, herbs and drugs, medical students were receiving no scientific training, and rarely saw any patients. At first, physicians considered surgery degrading, and continued to derive their prognoses from philosophy and astrology. In both the Old World and the New, the witch trials established male physicians on the side of the professions of law and theology, while women healers were relegated to the side of magic and evil.

What was life like for women in the earliest days of the American colonies? Is it possible that what occurred many generations ago could have any connection with woman and wife murder today? Ann Jones (1980, p. 21) provides some chilling facts. Jones, an expert on women in American history, states, "Women who settled in Massachusetts were probably the only English women who came to America before 1650 who came of their own volition. Most women were tricked or coerced. They did not emigrate. They were shipped." Women were exported. Single women were sent to be wives for the men in the New World for the purpose of making the colonies more settled, more permanent.

Tobacco in the New World was sometimes used to buy women from Europe. Englishmen had superfluous daughters, and in Protestant England extra daughters could no longer be sent to nunneries. In the New World a woman did not need a dowry to acquire a husband. Instead, she could be bought. In England, jobs for women were few, choice was often to become a wife or a whore unless a father continued to support the daughter.

Notorious English prisons were crowded with women, and hangings were frequent in the heavy-handed justice system. Women's crimes were often defined differently from crimes perpetrated by men. Often they were related to sexual activities or running away from home. Some of these women prisoners were undoubtedly glad to be exported to the colonies, a practice that continued until the time of the American Revolution when it became no longer possible. In the holds of ships, women prisoners were kept in chains, and many died during the two-month ocean crossing. Occasionally, women were sacrificed at sea to assuage storms supposedly caused by malevolent witches. Elizabeth Richard was executed for witchcraft in 1658 on a ship bound for Maryland. In 1659, records show that Katherine Grady was declared a witch and hanged at sea.

Between 1717 and 1721 Louisiana became home to 7,500 "unfortunates" from a Paris prison. Women could also come to the New World without paying for their passage by becoming servants. They would then be sold by shipowners and become indentured servants in the colonies for five to seven years. These women were a valuable commodity in the colonies where simply staying alive required a great deal of heavy, physical labor.

Men who bought and sold women for servants or wives took the profit but, as Jones states, many of the women fared better by the exchange than if they had remained in England. Marriage or servitude in America were often the only alternatives to prostitution, crime, or slow starvation in Europe. Women who sold themselves as wives, it was said, sold themselves only once or twice compared with prostitution.

As death frequently overtook both women and men in the colonies, there was a need for replacement spouses, thus enhancing women's value. Women in America were not seen as equal to men, but practicality required that the treatment of women be roughly equal to that of men. In the English doctrine of common law, women had become legally non-existent for all practical purposes. This "femme couvert" was set aside in the colonies, and in many localities women could vote and receive land allotments. Later, they lost some of their earlier autonomy. Equal treatment was not an unmixed blessing. In the colonies, the fornication law applied to both sexes, and men and women might receive an equal number of lashes or be fired and set on the gallows. Like men, women were pilloried and set in stocks, publicly whipped (often while being dragged through the streets), or forcibly held under water. In Virginia, they were dragged behind boats in the river and sometimes burned. Public whippings of women for petty offenses ended in 1750, but women might still be whipped for adultery or repeated bastardy. Not until 1800 did the public hangings finally end. In 1787 in New Haven, Connecticut, a 12-year-old girl was charged with murdering a six-year-old girl in a dispute over the ownership of strawberries. She was hanged in New London (Jones, 1980, p. 32).

Many women were hanged for suspected infanticide, sometimes making normal infant deaths a fearful event due to the possibility of women's consequent punishment. Although many infants died of illness, the discovery of a dead baby could lead to the suspicion of infanticide. Women had no control over their fertility, and the only available contraception was coitus interruptus, a method over which women had no control.

Servants were not allowed to marry, and if a female servant became pregnant she might receive a public whipping and extra years of servitude. If she attempted to get rid of the evidence by disposing of the fetus or child to avoid punishment, she might be hanged. A female servant could also be executed for concealing a suspected pregnancy.

Authority dictated that inferiors be required to submit full-time to superiors. Civil authority was based on this requirement. Patriarchs feared children's disobedience, servants' insolence, and wives' scolding, and the laws represented their fears. The commandment, to honor thy father, was invoked to enhance the subjugation of servant to master as well as the relationship of wife to husband. Women served God by serving their husbands. The Reverend Cotton Mather cautioned husbands against yoking wives too closely, and urged men to honor their wives.

English law of the 17th century gave husbands the right to chastise wives. However, the precarious Puritan colonies assigned that right to civil authorities. The state depended on a stable family life for its existence, and therefore took upon itself the mediation of family disputes, forbidding individual husbands to administer "stripes." Massachusetts took the lead in rigidly enforcing the law that forbade husbands to deliver bodily blows.

After the American Revolution, public punishments for domestic disputes were discontinued, and during the 1800s each man was expected to keep his own house in order. The famous "rule of thumb" meant that a man could hit his wife with a stick no thicker than his thumb. The reversion to an interpretation of English law authorized a husband to restrain a wife of her liberty and to administer moderate correction in case of "misbehavior." After the Revolution, women also lost property rights, rights to sue, and rights to possess their own bodies. Woman's duty was submission.

Did women ever kill men? Jones (1980) describes cases where this did occur. Nineteenth-century women were often trapped in marriages from which there was no escape, no divorce. Women who were injured and abused by drunken husbands did occasionally retaliate. Unequal to physical combat, the usual method was arsenic (the household product used for poisoning rats) although Lizzie Borden allegedly used an axe on her father and stepmother. If the crime were discovered and the wife convicted of causing her husband's death, the likely punishment was death. As with a dead infant, if a man succumbed without obvious cause, a woman could find herself unjustly suspected of her husband's murder.

During the 1800s, women's sphere became more constricted, more solitary. Their situation was cloistered even by European standards of the times. Men's and women's spheres became more differentiated, at home and in the workplace, and women were described by Jones as "dwindling into wives early in life." Women's work in the home was neither modernized nor recompensed, and women became empty-handed dependents. As the concept of the "lady" developed and leisure became possible for a woman who could afford it, the cult of female weakness and infirmity further reduced her power.

The Mississippi Supreme Court in 1824 ruled that a man had the right to chastise his wife moderately "without subjecting himself to vexatious prosecution for assault and battery, resulting in the discredit and shame of all parties concerned" (Jones, 1980, p. 283). By the middle of the nineteenth century, a North Carolina court ruled not only that chastisement was the husband's right but that the state had no business interfering unless "some permanent injury be inflicted or there be an excess of violence" (Jones, p. 284). Otherwise, the law was not to "invade the domestic forum or go behind the curtain" but rather to "leave the parties to themselves as the best mode of inducing them to make the matter up and live together as man and wife should" (Jones, p. 284).

However, toward the end of the 1800s the state laws began to change and to repudiate the precedents. In 1871, Massachusetts courts ruled that a man had no right to beat his wife and in the event of her death was guilty at least of manslaughter. Not until 1879 could murder in the first degree be found if a woman was killed by "beating, stamping, jumping, kicking" (Jones, p. 284).

By the second decade of the twentieth century, the courts found that society had progressed so much — as they described the situation — that a husband no longer needed a rod "to teach the wife her duty and her subjection. And the privilege, ancient though it be, to beat her with a stick, to pull her hair, choke her, spit in her face or kick her about the floor, or to inflict upon her other like indignities" was no longer "acknowledged by our law" (Jones, p. 284).

Wife beating was an unspoken issue behind nineteenth-century women's struggles for temperance, married women's property rights, liberalized divorce laws, child custody, and suffrage. The issues were not conceptualized as equality between the sexes. The unspoken problem was that women and children could be physically and sexually assaulted within the home.

Changing the laws did not mean that they would be enforced, or that behavior within the home would necessarily change. After women got the vote in 1918, much of the feminist agitation subsided. State laws specifically designated wife beating as an assault like any other assault although, in practice, the unofficial policy was to avoid interference in domestic matters. The issue did not surface again until the middle of the 1970s. Battered wives, their protection from the batterer, and their legal rights are now acknowledged problems that are only beginning to be adequately addressed. What remains unrecognized in the 1990s, and often denied even under overwhelming evidence, is that women are being murdered on a regular basis, and not by "bushy-haired intruders." Who done it? It was the husband!

MASTER OF THE HOUSEHOLD

With the above glimpse into American history and man's legal right to hit his woman until one hundred years ago, wife murder stories appear in a somewhat more understandable, if no less horrifying, perspective. It appears less surprising that Claus Von Bulow would accuse his now comatose wife of denying him sex after the birth of their daughter, Cosima, therefore giving him license to pursue other women. The testimony of the first trial is filled with Sunny's other supposed shortcomings in her role as a wife.

A woman obstetrician, 41 years old, was killed in Waltham, Massachusetts because her husband was jealous. The three paragraph news announcement (*Middlesex News*, Mar. 8, 1990) was brief and matter-of-fact.

The Central Park "preppy" murder of a young woman by her boyfriend was blamed on overly aggressive sex and was therefore excusable.

THE MAN WHO BUZZED BOSTON

"The Man Who Buzzed Boston" story received wide coverage while all but ignoring the fact that earlier in the day this man had killed his ex-wife!

At noon on May 9, 1989, Alfred Hunter, a 42-year-old, stocky, balding man, purchased 1,400 rounds of ammunition in a town near the New Hampshire border before appearing in Salem District Court to defend himself against assault charges brought by his ex-wife Elvira. Several times previously he had appeared on similar charges and was under a court restraining order to stay away from Elvira. His ex-wife was a 30-year-old woman from the Philippines. She told the judge that her husband had threatened to kill her if she did not drop the charges against him. Hunter calmly disputed his wife's story, and the judge sentenced him to a year of probation for violating the restraining order. He was ordered to report to the probation officer the following week.

At dusk that day, neighbors observed Hunter's car entering the street where his ex-wife lived in an apartment with their five-year-old son. At 9:30 p.m., smoke alarms went off in the fire station. Firemen found the apartment hallway filled with smoke and the smell of gunpowder. Neighbors had heard gunfire.

At 10:20 p.m. that evening at a nearby airport Hunter obtained a small private plane at gunpoint. At 10:40 p.m. Boston's Logan International Airport air traffic controllers saw the blip on their screen moving toward Boston and could get no response from the plane's pilot.

The red and white Cessna swooped over Fenway Park where the

Red Sox game had just ended. Cartridge casings from an AK-47 sprayed the pavement of nearby Kenmore Square. The plane then swept among Boston's skyscrapers and roared past police headquarters back toward the airport where it sprayed the Continental Airlines Terminal with bullets.

Heading back into the city, Hunter strafed narrow Boston streets and dipped the airplane under the Tobin Bridge. Hunter, a night worker for the Postal Service, headed for the post office building and repeatedly strafed the building, shooting out lights. The 1,200 postal workers took refuge in the basement. The plane flew low over Boston Harbor, no more than 20 feet away from a police patrol boat.

The airport as well as the major roadway leading into the city were closed. Messages went to all landing areas from Portland, Maine, to New York's La Guardia Airport to be on the look-out for the plane.

At 1 a.m., with the plane nearly out of fuel, Boston air traffic controllers saw the plane coming at them and could even see the white muzzle flashes of the AK-47. The order came, "Clear the tower." The plane headed out to sea, then returned to land on a runway and taxi toward the Delta Airlines terminal.

Alfred Hunter, motionless in the pilot's seat, was pulled from the plane. Seated at a table in an airport room, amidst the confusion he had created, he appeared quiet and innocuous. But few learned of Elvira's plight, her futile struggles for protection, his violation of the restraining order, and the fact that another woman had been murdered.

Violence against women is the most common and least reported crime. The roots of the problem go far back in time.

Chapter Three

"A Man's Home Is His Castle"

This old English proverb first appeared in print in 1851 in the writings of an English schoolmaster, Richard Mulcaster. It was Sir Edward Coke, the great defender of common law, who wrote in 1604, "The house of every man is his castle, and if thieves come to a man's house to rob or murder, and the owner or his servants kill any of the thieves in defense of himself and his house, it is no felony and he lose [sic] nothing." The king himself was prohibited from entering uninvited even the poorest and humblest cottage of one of his subjects (*Boston Globe*, Jan. 19, 1991).

A man's home is his castle. This dictum, with its countless repetitions, has expressed the dignity and rights of individuals and families in relation to the intervention and controls of community, society, and government. It affirms the sanctity of the home against unwanted intrusion, and it is to be breached only in the direst of circumstances.

No longer need a single woman marry to obtain rights to home ownership. Women (single or married) own property, have their own cars and their own medical insurance, go on their own vacations, and sometimes have substantial incomes. Wives are less likely to seek husbands' approval or "permission," before pursuing their own activities and interests. Yet many women still perceive a man to be the "head of the household," not recognizing male-female relationships founded on any other basis, and unaware of what this can mean in terms of their own potential vulnerability. Men continue to feel entitled to, and responsible for, the control of their wives' personal assets, including money that women either earn or bring to the relationship. Both members of the couple may be in apparent full agreement that his be so, whatever the reasons given.

19

Single women often express the desire to be married to "a man they can depend on." But what does this mean? How far can the limits of his control extend?

Often women's decision-making power is sharply limited and subject to his review. His control may include critical supervision of what she does, even giving orders and tracking much of what she does or says. He feels entitled to do this. Nor does she see anything extraordinary about what he does.

Women have traditionally taken the primary responsibility for "making the marriage work." They have long been expected to make more accommodations in marriage, or in any male-female relationship, than men. As society's nurturers and care-givers women have been charged with responsibility for man's happiness in the home, his comfort, and often the maintenance of his physical health.

However, women can also be vulnerable to blaming themselves without cause and accepting a disproportionate amount of guilt if they admit that they are unhappy or depressed. They can feel disloyal if they share their doubts or suffering with others, and many deny their discomfort even to themselves.

Marriage counselors in their practices see many women and few men come on their own initiative. The woman often attempts to persuade a reluctant husband to "accompany" her in order to protect his self-esteem. No one seems concerned about her self-esteem. The very fact that it is the woman who seeks professional counseling often reinforces her assumption, and his, that problems, if they exist at all, are her fault and that she must somehow fix them. She is the one who needs the professional help. He is content with the status quo. She is the one who is unhappy.

In addition, he may criticize her for bringing the family's problems to "outsiders," whether these resources be physicians, psychologists, religious counselors, or the police. The words used may be, "airing the family laundry in public," thereby placing still another burden on a woman attempting to solve problems. She is to keep the secrets.

Man's role as woman's protector has undeniable appeal. The desire to be "taken care of" is often strong, and nurturance is universally sought throughout life by both sexes. Men have long been expected to acknowledge their dependence only in specific ways involving the services women have traditionally provided.

Because employment and school environments are frequently experienced as competitive and self-seeking, both sexes want to see the home as a sanctuary from the world of the marketplace. Her role has been to please him, with his traditional role that of protecting her.

Women may not recognize that, in some men, what masquerades as protectiveness sometimes has the potential for coercive and demeaning encounters which are the antithesis of either love or protection. The hero in the musical *The King and I* sings his song, musing about the risks of outside influences to his country, "Might they not protect me out of all I own?"

Expectations about man's authority over his home still exist in state laws. Wives may be required to live in the locale the husband selects; the assumption being, of course, that his economic responsibility requires this.

Men regularly deny problems within the home despite obvious evidence, relying on the fact that what occurs within the home may not be easily corroborated. Wives' testimony may be discounted. Also, in still largely male courts of law, there is frequently discomfort with the idea that a woman could be disloyal to her husband by publicly accusing him of anything.

Men may even be accused of murdering their wives and yet still seek custody of their children. Richard Crafts sought custody, although he did not receive it after he was convicted of murder. It is not uncommon that despite intense efforts of assaulted wives, other family members, and the testimony of medical experts, violent men obtain custody, even sole custody. It is this threat that has influenced many women living with dangerous men to remain in the relationship.

Parents maintain authority over their children. Mothers often defer to fathers over what constitutes appropriate control and discipline. The phrase "raising a child" implies an active parental responsibility in this regard. Parents, especially fathers, have the right to punish. All manner of parental behaviors are condoned in the name of discipline, including hitting (spanking), shouting, physical coercion [yanking, pulling, pushing, insults, threats, and physical con-

finement ("stay in your room," "you're grounded for a week")],
and various forms of deprivation such as cutting off financial resources and contact with peers. Parental controls, including those
that go far beyond what many would consider appropriate parental
responses, are often presented to children as "love" and "caring
what happens to you."

Children appear at schools with bruises and at hospitals with
burns or broken bones. The parental explanation is most often that
the observable injury is the result of an accident. When does "discipline" become child abuse? Or child murder? In many states, suspected child abuse requires mandatory reporting to authorities.
However, teachers and physicians often express reluctance to pursue problems occurring within the home, even when they have reason to suspect a problem.

In their 1990 meeting, the National Association of Social Workers, which had previously opposed corporal punishment in schools,
passed a resolution discouraging physical discipline within the
home. It was passed as a policy rather than a blueprint for legislation. "The vast majority of child abuse incidents start out with parents thinking they are disciplining the child," stated the staff director of the Association's Commission on Education. "Beating,
whipping, or spanking is not a rational way of teaching a child how
to change his or her behavior" (*Middlesex News*, 1990). Many experts have long stated that hitting a child models a form of behavior
the child will repeat.

When "a man's home is his castle" and his economic power is
largely responsible for maintaining the roof over a family's heads,
the attitude that a father's needs usually take priority over other
family members' needs is hardly surprising. The message is, "Do
not disturb him. Do not upset him. He knows what is best. Keep the
peace. Be grateful." No matter what he does, the message continues, "He *is* your father." This tradition enables behavior that
elsewhere would constitute a crime—an assault or felony—to be
more easily ignored if it occurs within the family.

A woman escorting her children to a bus stop (McCarthy, 1991),
was followed down the street by her estranged husband. He pleaded
with her to allow him to accompany her, despite their separation.
Shortly before, he had come, uninvited, to the home, and the es-

tranged wife had made him the sandwich he requested. Appearing calm and controlled, and in full view of passers-by as well as his children, he knifed the woman seventeen times and left her dead in the bushes. He tossed away the knife, saying, "I hope I killed her." The bus driver who witnessed the attack closed the doors and honked the horn, saying to his passengers, "This looks like a domestic. I don't want to get involved."

Neighbors are often reluctant to interfere or to call for help. Several days passed before Helle Crafts's fellow flight attendants stopped trying to get answers about her whereabouts from her husband and reported her disappearance to the police. Although she had told several of her friends, "If anything happens to me, don't think it was an accident," they still hesitated.

When women fear themselves to be in imminent danger and call the police, the response until recently has often been less than satisfactory. Police reports read "family fight" or "domestic violence." The man is given the chance to walk around the block to "cool off." Crime in the home is only beginning to receive the professional attention that similar crimes committed elsewhere receive.

WOMEN'S SERVICES

Women's vulnerability is increased when the spouse's assumption, and requirement, is that she provide services according to the traditional model. Otherwise his response may range from questioning disapproval to violent rage. Not one room in the house may be really "hers." Yet, if the home is her job and she doesn't do it, or doesn't do it "right," a woman can become vulnerable to her own guilt as well as her husband's commands. She can never be sure she is doing enough even to meet her own expectations. Sometimes a husband, deprived of expected services including sexual services, will verbally attack, physically attack, or even rape his woman without feeling any guilt. Instead, he will feel entitled to "set his house in order."

"WEARING THE PANTS"

Shakespeare's play *The Taming of the Shrew* portrays a view of male prerogative that is seemingly incongruent with today's values. However, words used to describe positive male characteristics may have a different cast when applied to women. He may be aggressive, persevering, achieving. She will be "pushy," domineering, refusing to "let it go," overreacting, or even hysterical. If she persists in attempting to set standards of what is acceptable to her, she may be described as "nagging." She may blame herself, trying to be more accepting and less demanding. What has been described as a feminine role is more often that of a second-class citizen.

If submissiveness becomes the female role, the woman becomes less able to protect the children from abuse. With her own loss of self-respect, and if not treated respectfully by her husband, she may lose the respect of her children. In some families, the woman seems to have almost as little power in the home as the children. Young male children, despite their pain at the way their mothers are treated, risk growing up to be violent toward women and children.

The Wolsieffer case has been the topic of countless columns in the Wilkes-Barre (Pennsylvania) *Times Leader*. In 1986, Glenn Wolsieffer, a graduate of Georgetown Dental School, allegedly strangled his wife Betty. He claims the murder resulted from an intruder entering the apartment. Just before her death, Betty told a friend that she was finally going to confront her husband about his affair with another woman. In fact, she was planning to discuss it with him the very evening she was killed. Those investigating the case hypothesize from what is known about their relationship, that, by standing up to her husband, she had given him (in his mind) cause for violence. By trying to interfere with his life, she may have challenged his authority, with the result that she lost her life. No one knows what really happened that night. Dr. Wolsieffer was finally convicted of Betty's murder, largely as a result of the investigative work done by Ken Corbett of the *Times Leader*. While the trim, dark-haired Dr. Wolsieffer's case is being appealed he continues to practice dentistry in Arlington, Virginia. Although admitting his affair with another woman, he denies murdering his wife. Ironically, Ken Corbett is accused of obtaining some of the information leading to the conviction through illegal wire-tapping. Dr. Wolsieffer may yet go free.

FEMALE DEPENDENCY AND "THE CULT OF FEMALE WEAKNESS"

There are other aspects of learned female dependency that go back into history. During colonial days in America, the family unit maintained a high degree of self-sufficiency in producing its own food, clothing, and household goods. Women cared for the sick in their homes and assisted in the care of the sick in the homes of neighbors.

When industrialization took men from their homes to work at jobs, women became increasingly isolated for much of their days. At the same time, women of class had the leisure to avoid much of the physical labor of earlier women settlers. Stylish women endured corsetry, shoes, and clothing that tended to inhibit their physical activity.

Athletic activities were part of women's lives only in the most limited ways, and women were expected never to compete with men. If they had more than minimal ability in lawn tennis or rowing, they learned to conceal their prowess. Women with mysterious feminine ailments were often prescribed the "rest cure" by their physicians. Those who sank into "malaise" or depression might also receive this prescription. Today's health and fitness movement has reversed many earlier assumptions about women's frailty, although many still express fear of unfeminine "bulging muscles." A few women have become proficient in martial arts, largely as a means of self-defense and self-protection against crime in the streets.

The nineteenth-century "cult of female weakness" included the intellect. The belief was widely held that excessive use of the intellect interfered with female reproductive functions. It was thought that woman was ruled by her uterus, and early medical textbooks warned against using her mind excessively. Women should avoid the stress of too much study, and free themselves of the worries of the marketplace and the aspirations of entering the professions. The penalty of pursuing manly vocations of law or medicine might be female ailments and reproductive troubles. There was also the added penalty of the unhappy likelihood of becoming a spinster (Solomon, 1985).

OUTSIDE THE "CASTLE": WOMEN AND DEPENDENCE ON MEDICAL PROFESSIONALS

Women's dependency on male physicians began during the eighteenth and nineteenth centuries. During the nineteenth century, the healers and midwives serving women were almost eradicated, largely because middle-class men aspired to medicine as a prestige profession. Women, with one or two notable exceptions, could neither study nor practice medicine. Becoming a nurse was the only available alternative, and nurses' status and pay remained low. Nurses had little input into the medical care system. Men sought a market for their medical services and women became their major market.

At first, for reasons of modesty, women of class resisted using male physicians. Male doctors delivered babies under the voluminous skirts of their patients, using only their sense of touch, and with the woman facing away from the doctor. Charity patients in hospitals had no choice, and could therefore be used as teaching material for aspiring doctors. Dr. Sims developed his gynecological procedures on unanesthetized slave women.

Men had tools for medical treatment, some of which they brought back from their European travels. They obtained forceps which were used to expedite birth, whether or not these instruments were needed. Midwives had no access to this tool. Other medical treatments included placing leeches on the cervix of the uterus, introducing mercury compounds into the uterus, removing ovaries (sometimes seen as the source of women's "orneriness"), and operating on the uterus.

Men who provided medical treatment became the source of women's instruction about their own bodies. Healthy childbirth ceased to be a normal biological process. It was redefined as a medical condition requiring routine intervention and treatment. The medical procedures used often had the potential to place healthy women and babies at risk. Women lost an important part of their female identity when they lost their role as experts in giving birth and stopped assisting other women during childbirth.

When doctors delivered babies, childbirth infections were frequent and often fatal. They occurred because physicians were in contact with infectious patients and then attended childbirth without washing their hands. Dr. Semmelweiss in Austria had identified this problem during the mid-nineteenth century, but his findings were ridiculed and ignored.

The hospital environment of the twentieth century, with its crowded conditions and sick patients, provided additional risk of infection. "Staph" infections continue to be a problem in hospital births. However, when women gave birth at home with midwives and neighbors in attendance, childbed fever was almost non-existent. Nevertheless, having a doctor deliver one's baby, at home or in the hospital, became a status symbol.

When women moved to the hospital to give birth, they did so not for reasons of safety – in fact, statistics showed the opposite – but to obtain the new "twilight sleep." Hospitals advertised in women's magazines, proclaiming that hospital birth was the modern way. Women could go to sleep for the birth, have their babies taken care of in the nursery, and other women helping in the home would not even have to do the laundry after childbirth (Bean, 1990; Wertz and Wertz, 1989)!

Hospitals had feared that women of means would be unwilling to come to hospitals to give birth because initially only charity cases (women who had no homes) used hospitals for childbirth. But, as women had accepted male physicians, they were also persuaded to have their babies in hospitals.

The "twilight sleep" resulted in women who were unconscious, amnesic, and immobilized. They were lined up in common labor rooms, restrained in their beds, and under the influence of mysterious drugs that had never been proven safe for women or babies. Minutes before birth, women were moved to delivery rooms. Their legs were tied into stirrups and they were handcuffed to the delivery table with stout leather straps. Spinal or gas anesthesia was superimposed on drugs already administered.

After "delivery," the newborns were immediately trundled to a nursery where they were lined up in rows. Babies were largely inaccessible to both parents for the duration of the hospital stay. They were brought to mothers on a strict schedule, usually accompanied by a bottle, and collected as soon as possible after they were fed.

Both women and men were overpowered by institutional needs as well as their loss of knowledge about normal birth, unrealistic fears of pain, newborn baby care and postpartum care. They lacked the support of other knowledgeable women. A woman in the 1970s said, "I felt as though I wasn't invited to my own delivery" (Bean, 1982, p. 213). She, and others, continue to see childbirth as part of the violence against women.

Today's women continue to express fear of "not getting to the hospital on time." If their babies arrive unexpectedly at home, they often blame themselves as though they have done something "wrong"! With all the birthing rooms and family participation during birth, women can still be disempowered during the profound female experience of giving birth. Most, even those attending Lamaze classes, do not know they have the power to refuse unproven routine hospital technology, nor are they aware of its potential risks.

From the beginning of women's dependence on male physicians, doctors saw their female patients frequently because of women's ability to reproduce. Without training, it followed that doctors became counselors on family life and female sexuality, including wifely responsibilities and their patients' role as women. Ivan Illich (1976) decried the medicalization of normal life events such as birth, child development, adolescence, sexuality, menopause, and dying. These perceptions of medical omnipotence were reflected in obstetrical textbooks as late as the 1970s. Many women, long after the publication of the widely read *Our Bodies, Ourselves*, still see their gynecologists as authority figures beyond the realm of appropriate gynecologic expertise.

As women have become trained as physicians in growing numbers, there has been the expectation, as yet largely unfulfilled, that the medical doctor might assume a role of one among several consultants, rather than an authority figure requiring patient compliance. There is also the expectation that women physicians better understand female issues and problems, including those related to male violence against women. Medical education and training, however, remains largely male-dominated. Women's health organizations have alerted the public to controversies regarding contraceptive advice, female surgery, and childbirth practices (the 25% cesarean rate, for example). However, women still have a high degree of dependency on traditionally trained male physicians for female problems. And medical authority continues its tendency to follow the model of patriarchal authority.

WOMEN AND THE CHILD CARE EXPERTS

Beginning in the 1920s, women, already dependent on male physicians, found that a new expert, also male, had arrived to take care of their children's health. The new expert on children was the pediatrician. His expertise went beyond childhood medical problems, vitamins, and immunizations. He gave authoritative advice on discipline, nutrition, sleep patterns, toilet training, feeding, and even how often to feed babies. He set up a "schedule" for mothers to follow.

Infant formula, heavily marketed to pediatricians and mothers, began to pre-empt breastfeeding. Pediatricians could not assist mothers with breastfeeding, but they were indeed prepared to prescribe infant formula. If a formula caused infant distress, the pediatrician could readjust it until satisfactory. Women learned that bottle feeding was the modern way, and that what their mothers had done was "old fashioned." Young women were advised to listen to the pediatrician, to follow the schedule regardless of the baby's cries, and to ignore "old wives' tales." What appeared as a way of freeing women — the infant formula and the schedule — actually disempowered them.

Isolated for much of the day in their homes, women anticipated scheduled pediatrician visits as opportunities to talk about their babies and learn about child care. They did not know that none of this information was included in either the medical school curriculum or the subsequent pediatric residency training.

While women sought fulfillment in motherhood, they also learned that mothers could "spoil" their children. Sons, in particular, could be "smothered" by mothering. It was very hard for women to know when they were doing a good job because they were no longer the experts.

WOMEN AS OBJECTS

Much has been written about women's bodies as objects that are used to market everything from cars to soap. Often the attempt is to find an error in her body to "fix" with a new hairstyle, different outfits, or a new diet. The concern is not woman's right and desire to be beautiful, to decorate herself as she wishes, and create the image she wishes to portray. The concern is rather that studies show so many women to be unnecessarily dissatisfied with the way they look or with trying to follow images promoted by advertisers.

Women with even a few pounds of extra weight often experience loss of self-esteem, feeling vulnerable to self-criticism as well as male criticism. The extra weight is experienced as possibly signifying the woman's weakness, lack of self-discipline, or inability to stick to a plan. Even as they feel criticized for being fat, some dieting women report that their husbands act in ways to sabotage their diets, even to the point of bringing home tempting sweets and high-calorie foods. Behaviorists explain this phenomenon as the man feeling threatened by his woman's determination to control her eating. She might gain power in other ways, even leave him for another man. She would certainly become less vulnerable to his criticism.

The pornography trade exploits woman's body as sex object and woman as helpless, and even willing, victim of male lust and aggression. Here woman is possessed, conquered, subjugated. Her body is used for entertainment that features humiliation, physical pain, and even injury. Violence against women is presented in the context of male sexual gratification. Many strongly resist media censorship, perceiving the issue as one of restricting artistic freedom, but others question why this freedom includes presenting male subjugation of women as entertainment.

The objective of the rapist has been found to be that of acting out his aggression against women, with sex being used to dominate and humiliate women. And the male myth is still believed, that women may enjoy the role of victim.

With these portrayals, if a crime is committed against a woman, might it not merely be seen as male violence gone too far? As in the Central Park Preppie Murder? In fact, it may not be recognized as a crime at all.

The Rhode Island Rape Crisis Center surveyed 1,700 sixth- to ninth-grade students. They were asked (without using the word rape) under what circumstances a man has the right to kiss or have sexual intercourse with a woman against her will. Results showed that 65% of the boys and 57% of the girls said it was acceptable for a man to force a woman to have sex if they have been dating for more than six months (*The Washington Post*, May 6, 1988. Reprinted by the Rhode Island Rape Crisis Center in Providence.)

THE PATRIARCHY AND THE RISKS TO WOMEN

Patriarchy in our society is so ingrained that it is often barely recognized by men or women. It is not a question of who opens doors or who pays the check, or the courtesies of interpersonal relationships.

Weiss (1990) found in his study of suburban men holding middle-management jobs that it is easier to have a "non-traditional" marriage before children arrive. Men feel responsible for their families whether or not their wives work. Men depend on their wives to make a home for them and their children. The men in his study wanted to be successful enough to be able to give their wives the opportunity to choose between working or staying home.

Shaevitz and Shaevitz (1980) report men fear their wives' work to be more important to their wives than their careers or themselves. Many men remain unsure about an equal, reciprocal partnership and even as they attempt this, they expect their wives to play the same roles as their mothers did. Expressive caring is often difficult for men, who are also unsure of what women want. And men seldom feel able to sacrifice their careers for equal parenting.

The literature considers women's choices in today's society: the submissiveness of the traditional marital role in which women minister to the family's needs ahead of their own, the world of work, or the independent life and the inevitable ticking of the biological clock. What is woman's identity: wife, mother, housekeeper, employee? How to balance? How to avoid guilt at what is left undone? Can she do it all? Men, too, can be exploited by their women and stressed by their work. Men, too, may be unsure of their family roles in the changing contemporary society.

Sexist attitudes and behaviors may provide the milieu for relationships in which women, their bodies, and their reproductive processes can be treated as property to be controlled by others, both inside the "castle" and outside the "castle." *Because these attitudes and behaviors so closely mirror the known risk factors for woman murder, women and society may be blind to dangers that would otherwise be clearly visible.*

Chapter Four

The Ties That Bind

The following true story represents many others. It illustrates almost the entire range of risk factors described in the following chapters. Almost every woman in this puzzling abyss feels that she is alone, yet it is the common story.

Anita is a hospital medical assistant who has been married to Donald for two years. She claims she loves him. She continues to try to gain his approval despite her consistent "failures" to accomplish this for any sustained period of time. She steps up her approval-seeking behavior in her desperate effort to make this marriage work. Sometimes Donald tells her their problems are her fault. At other times, he accuses her of imagining them and of being a complainer.

Donald was Anita's first and only serious boyfriend in high school. Her parents have no idea what is happening to their daughter. Because they never really liked Donald or approved of the marriage, Anita feels extra pressure to prove them wrong and to make the marriage work. Her pride makes her unwilling to risk her precarious adult standing by admitting to herself that she has marriage problems and that possibly she has made a mistake. There is no turning back. No one must know. She and Donald must work things out. Things will get better. They love each other.

Being unhappy only reinforces her diminishing self-esteem. Arriving at work tear-stained, often with bruises on her arm, is humiliating. Her co-workers try to avoid acknowledging that anything is out of the ordinary and try to avoid intruding on her private life. Not knowing what to say, they also tend to leave her more, rather than less, alone with her unhappiness. Several times a day, Donald calls Anita at work, demanding to talk to his wife and informing the receptionist that the call is urgent. Finally her co-workers inquire what is going on with Donald. Over the next several weeks the story gradually unfolds.

Anita is trying to lose weight to avoid Donald's comments about how "ugly" she is when she is fat. She attempts to restrict her diet, with little success, to lose those ten pounds, hoping that then he will stop criticizing and hurting her. Despite her diet, Donald demands that she continue to prepare tasty meals for him.

Anita buys the groceries and pays the rent because Donald has not yet found a satisfactory job. He reminds her that he followed her to the military base from their midwest hometown, as though this is somehow another of her failings as a wife. It seems to occur to neither that Anita is Donald's meal ticket.

Anita tries to avoid upsetting him, attempting to find out what she is doing "wrong" to "stir him up." She keeps an eye on his face and body language, searching without success for clues to impending outbursts. Sometimes he breaks a plate. At home, Anita has become very quiet, saying little. Weekends are the worst.

When invited to social events, even a wedding, on the military base, she often cancels at the last minute without explanation. She says something about Donald being unable to come.

One evening, the situation at the apartment gets so bad that Anita leaves to stay with a friend on the military base. Donald calls her repeatedly at the friend's apartment, apologizing for his behavior and begging her to come home. He tells her that he loves her and that from now on everything will be all right. Next day, she goes home. Within a few days, things are not all right and getting worse. Now the blame is on Anita for leaving. He says she brought it on herself.

At work, Anita is informed about battered women's shelters, but she finds the idea humiliating. It would force her to confront danger from her own husband. What would people say? To admit failure? To leave her dreams, her marriage, and her wedding presents for a shelter? This does not fit with anything she knows, and she finds it hard to acknowledge to herself that Donald could hurt her, even though he already has. He constantly professes his love and need for her, promising that he will never hurt her again. Now Donald has another complaint: she doesn't want to sleep with him anymore, and he seems to have no idea why. Doesn't she love him? He is angry and, once again, Anita feels guilty.

In two weeks, Anita's parents are coming for a visit and she is in a panic. She hopes for a peaceful interlude so that she won't have any bruises on her arms when they arrive. If she has injuries, she hopes they will not be visible. Why is her marriage not working when she is trying so hard?

Finally she agrees to leave Donald and the apartment, but she feels guilty and alone. Donald's calls at her workplace increase in number to a dozen or more a day, begging her to come back. She learns that he used to get hit as a child, and he wants her sympathy. She is tempted, but decides to wait.

When she does not comply with his wishes that she come home immediately, he persuades her to let him meet her after work. He then drives Anita to a secluded place, telling her that they need to "talk." He returns her safely, but these after-work drives continue. The pressure on her to return is constant and escalating. Anita sees this attention as evidence of his "love." She suggests that the two of them go to counseling, but he says it is unnecessary. Anita wants to go. He therefore feels justified in seeing the problem as hers, not his. She doesn't really want to go alone and is uncertain about making the commitment. Besides, it is hard to admit the problem. Perhaps things will get better. She hopes so. Donald is adamant that there will be no divorce, no separation from his wife.

Anita is transferred to another duty station and Donald follows. Before she leaves for new duty she is warned to live in a secure area and not to give Donald her address, but she just can't do that to Donald. He is her husband. Anita is in real danger of permanent injury, even death. His persistent control over Anita, including his violence, is being rewarded every time he exhibits it. She wants to believe that his possessiveness and punishments are signs that he cares about her. He says he wants her to get pregnant, but so far she has resisted pregnancy "until things are more settled." Her fantasy is that she will finally gain Donald's approval and have a happy home and children. More likely, according to statistics and the available information, is that she will receive permanent injuries. No one has informed her that she is at risk of being murdered by the man she says she loves.

The warning signs in this story are many. Anita may have a fatal "accident" that will never be properly investigated. It is even possible that she will simply disappear and that no one will ever know what happened.

When the estranged husband of the Brandeis University employee chased her down and shot her in the university cafeteria, his reason was that he "loved" her so much he didn't want to let her go.

Experts working with violent men cannot predict with certainty which men will kill. A social worker describes, with dismay, a man she treated. His therapy was court-mandated because of his periodic violence against his lover, a nightclub entertainer. The social worker thought that she had formed a successful therapeutic relationship with this man and was of the opinion that he was making real progress. Several weeks later her professional confidence was shattered when her radio-alarm clock woke her with a news story about her client. During the night he had killed his lover.

CAN THIS BE LOVE?

Men and women, for reasons rooted in past experiences, sometimes accept behaviors as love which appear on a rational level as the very antithesis of love. Violent, even painful, sex is portrayed as "love." Jealousy can be seen as evidence of "love." Controlling what she does, keeping her ignorant of family affairs, and even giving her "household money" is presented as protective and caring. Coercive behaviors are "for her own good" or "to teach her a lesson."

As late as 1978, Jones (1980) describes the case of an ex-wife who was beaten, kicked, raped, and killed. There was no question about "who done it," but the Kansas prosecutor stated, "he didn't mean to kill her. He just meant to give her a good thumping!" This implies a husband's legitimate authority that is not entirely inconsistent with his love for his family.

Could not a better definition of love include partnership, satisfying communication, mutual attraction, desire to please one other, and mutual respect? Would it not include wanting what is best for the other person and giving that person freedom, autonomy, and opportunity for growth and enhancement of self-esteem? Many men and women have never experienced this kind of love or had any sustained exposure to a loving relationship, either as children or adults. Forward (1986) discusses "toxic parenting": wives and children hit with belts, verbally demeaned, molested, and subjected to the inappropriate and unpredictable behaviors of substance-addicted adults. There may be coldness, criticism, and neglect of physical and emotional needs of family members. Women and children may be subjugated to the point where every part of their lives falls under male review and control. And all this may be explained with the phrase "because I love you."

Other factors operate in "love gone wrong." Woman as property. Woman as object. The male image of responsibility, control, and dominance — all of which discourage men from revealing feelings and emotions other than anger. Even unbridled expressions of anger including shouting, and possibly lashing out physically at people or objects, are often tolerated in men. Women still react to feminine role expectations of submission to male dominance by admiring "strong men." The media portrayal of love is commonly the antithesis of a romantic, loving, or truly sexual relationship. The hero seduces and conquers the woman and "sweeps her off her feet," — leaving the door open for coercion and victimization of women.

As Gillespie (1989) says, women are not exposed to physical fighting, do not expect it, and are not prepared for it. Boys are not expected to hit girls, and girls do not hit girls. Therefore, Anita is at a loss for how to respond to physical assault.

Anita thinks she "loves" Donald and he thinks he "loves" her. She thinks he loves her because he says so and gives her so much, albeit unwanted, attention. Donald has become fearful that she is seeing another man and his jealousy, too, is seen by both as evidence of his "love" for her. Her tears and increased efforts to lose weight and make everything "right" for Donald are also seen by them both as "love."

Donald needs his wife to maintain his self-esteem and to provide the services to which he feels entitled, including the money Anita earns and which he manages. Anita needs, for her own self-respect, to make the marriage work. But Donald is angry and Anita is in the deepest profound pain. Their "love" is not warm, nourishing, or trusting. It is demeaning and downright dangerous. When "love" includes such pain, it is a caricature of love, if that. So-called love has included mutilation murder, rape murder, battery murder, historical immolation of women "witches," and "honor crimes." In some Latin and Middle Eastern countries, women who are believed to have lost their virginity are sometimes killed by their relatives. A Saudi Arabian princess was recently executed for committing adultery.

THE NUMBERS

In 1988, the number of U.S. women murdered by their husbands was 1,075. Boyfriends murdered an additional 517, making the total number 1,592. The statistics have varied little over the past several years, but most experts agree that the number is underreported, and that the number of wife and female partner murders cannot be accurately determined. The FBI estimates that one-third of all women homicide victims between 1976 and 1987 were murdered by husbands or ex-husbands (National Institute of Justice, 1990; Fact Sheet on Domestic Violence Murders). However, The National Woman Abuse Prevention Project Report on Understanding Domestic Violence (1990, p. 9) places the true number at 52%, far higher than FBI statistics. This means that more than half of all women murdered are victims of husbands, ex-husbands, or lovers.

Homicide can be the end result of male control over women. It may, or may not, be the final result of a series of assaults taking place in the home. Because it is estimated that only one in ten violent incidents is reported, the problem of correlating past assaults to murder is compounded. Some dangerous men abuse their wives psychologically instead of physically; they may do both. A further complication in compiling statistics results because the number of wife or partner murders remains underreported to agencies compiling statistics. A woman is beaten in her home every 15 seconds in the United States (National Coalition Against Domestic Violence, Fact Sheet, 1991). Violence in the home is the single largest cause of injury to women in the United States. The end result may be death.

Chapter Five

Danger — How to Know?

Experts cannot predict who will be killed. Each woman is usually alone in assessing her risk. She is in the best position to note the "markers" in his behavior at home that could indicate danger. It is better to talk about them with knowledgeable professionals and other experts than to ignore them and make "the best of a bad situation." The murder may be committed with no obvious warning signs, and when researching prior contributory factors, the story is necessarily incomplete because the victim is dead.

Police define assault as the use of an object — including fist or shod foot, club, knife, or gun — to hit the victim. How many women who have been threatened or injured by husbands or boyfriends will die?

Not all killers are caught and convicted. For example, there is the Brian Simoni case. Maybe he is innocent, and maybe not. Police consider him their prime suspect and are convinced they will find the evidence they need. "It's his first murder. It's not *our* first murder." However, in gathering evidence, the first 20 minutes at the crime scene are the most important, and more than a year has passed. Simoni's lawyer demands that his client either be charged or exonerated.

Brian Simoni, a tall, thin man with a dark mustache, lives with his three children in Norwood, Massachusetts. He owns a garden shop. Just before Christmas in 1989 his attractive and vivacious wife was killed by two shots fired in a nearby shopping mall. She was found dead in her Jeep in the mall's parking lot. The robbery motive has been discounted. Her husband turned his gun over to police; it was found to not be the gun that had killed his wife.

The couple were said to have been having marital and financial difficulties. When the murder occurred, the Simonis were only days away from divorce, a time known to be risky for women. Nothing more is known about this case.

Willis Brown, an American Airlines pilot, appeared to Regina and to her family as a real "catch." He is tall, handsome, urbane, and has been described as "brilliant." To the outside world, the Browns gave the appearance of being the perfect couple. After their marriage, in rapid succession Willis and Regina had three children. Even Regina's parents, the Fontenots in Texas, had no idea that there was anything wrong with the marriage until after she disappeared. The Browns had been estranged for months, but her parents discovered the problems only after she disappeared.

The Brown home—in an upscale neighborhood on Whipporwill Road in Newtown, Connecticut—was only one and one half miles from the Crafts' home, the scene of the "woodchipper murder." Four months after Helle Crafts disappeared from her home, also in the middle of the night, Regina disappeared. However, Regina's body has never been found, and therefore there is no proof that she was murdered.

At approximately 2 a.m. on the night Regina disappeared a neighbor called the police to complain about a barking dog in the Brown home. The dispatcher said, "We can't do anything . . . Call the dog officer in the morning." No police car was dispatched to the home that night. Because no body has yet been found, Regina remains listed as a missing person. The clues were few. Fortunately, Regina had a friend to whom she had earlier confided that she was terrified of Willis. On the evening of her disappearance Regina called her friend to say, "Don't talk, just listen . . . it's dark, I'm in danger. If my parents haven't heard from me in two days, be alarmed. Willis will have done to me what he promised." It is only this final message that has kept the case open (Pilot's Wife, 1991).

Left behind were her purse, all her clothes, and a one-thousand dollar check. One of her children drew a picture in school of his mother being choked by his father "and she was blue and she fell down." The drawing of an apparent attack on his mother is the only known warning sign. Being choked is indeed a risk factor for becoming a murder victim! Willis's threat to his wife, as presented in Regina's last telephone call, is a clear warning sign.

Willis shows no apparent concern about his wife's fate and continues his unbelievable tale about his wife being a "coke addict." This story only heightens suspicion of Willis's involvement in her disappearance. Her husband remains the chief suspect, but because no body has yet been found, Willis continues to fly for American Airlines.

Kenneth Z. Taylor's story is described in a later chapter. Taylor, an Indiana dentist, had three wives. With each succeeding marriage his treatment of them became worse. He abandoned his first wife without warning or explanation just days before she gave birth. He tried to chloroform the second wife. He murdered his third wife. The escalation of violence is a warning sign, but his third wife, Teresa, had no knowledge of the previous wives' fate.

In the puzzling Carol Stuart case, the warning signs — as far as is known — were few, but even here they are known to have existed. About a month before his wife's murder, Charles told a friend that he wanted his wife "done away with." He said he felt he was "losing control" and that Carol was "getting the upper hand" in the relationship now that she was pregnant. Unfortunately, Charles's conversation with his friend was not relayed anywhere else. And if it had, the outcome would likely have been no different. No one would have known what to do.

Sharon Gordon (39) of Marlborough, Massachusetts, knew she was at risk. In January, 1989, a year after her marriage to David Robbins (41) she obtained a court restraining order to keep David away from the apartment. She obviously feared violence. Did she know she might die?

At the trial, four witnesses stated that Robbins frequently threatened to harm his wife. Sharon had sought a restraining order, claiming that "He says he will kill and really hurt me only when he is drinking. And when he is like this I am afraid of what he will do to my daughter and myself." Four months earlier she requested an emergency order claiming that her husband had hit her, verbally abused her, and threatened to harm her (*Middlesex News*, Dec. 5, 1990).

After her death, neighbors said that, despite the court restraining orders, Sharon had periodically allowed him back into the apartment. Sharon was slain the morning after she had ordered David out of the apartment for good during an argument over the checkbook. Forcible separation without adequate police protection, including powerful legal consequences for violation of the restraining order, placed Sharon's life in jeopardy. At 4:05 a.m. on April 18, 1990, police responded to a neighbor's call and found Sharon on the floor near the bathroom of her ground-level apartment. A short time later, David was found with blood on him.

The weapon was a knife taken from another woman's apartment. He used the knife to cut the screen of the door, and a stolen key to gain entrance. He arrived at about 3:30 a.m. because he knew Sharon would be getting ready to leave for her job as manager of the doughnut shop in a nearby town. While Sharon was in the shower, he slashed her throat and stabbed her 14 times in the neck, face, arms, and back. He then left her to bleed to death in front of her thirteen-year-old daughter and her daughter's friend.

Her daughter, Nicolette, testified in court that she was awakened at about 4 a.m. by a scream. She ran out of her room and found her mother standing in the kitchen leaning against a counter so she would not fall and "mumbling something," but her daughter could not understand her. Her mother was bleeding heavily, mostly from her neck and face. Sharon then fell to the floor in a pool of blood. David came into the kitchen from the bathroom, and when his stepdaughter attempted to go to her mother he "took my arms and threw me. I hit the wall." An upstairs neighbor testified that he had heard "screaming not like you ever heard on television . . . something I never want to hear again."

David's lawyer blamed Sharon's murder on David's long history of drug and alcohol abuse. Because he had been drinking, the claim was made that he was not responsible for what he did to Sharon. This, even though he had earlier told his sister-in-law, "If I can't have Sharon, no one can." This was a clear warning sign. Despite the prior problems, only *after* the murder was he sent to a state hospital for evaluation of his drug and alcohol problem. However, the violence problem remained unaddressed.

Sometimes no warning signs are available to those investigating a murder case, and no evidence to gain a conviction.

For example, in 1990, Carol Marie Dubuisson, mother of a six-year-old daughter, was found dead by her landlord and another friend who entered the apartment. They smelled the strong odor of decay, and found Carol's body stuffed into the chimney of her fireplace along with her bloody mattress. The landlord said, "Whoever killed her stuffed her in a hole so small it was unbelievable." A woman in the apartment above Carol reported "hearing loud music and a boom" during the night of November 25th.

The murdered woman's daughter was taken to another home by Carol's boyfriend. She may have witnessed the murder. She asked her foster mother, "Is my mother still in the chimney?" Police charged Carol's boyfriend, who had been living in the same apartment, with "unlawful disposal of her body." He is a suspect, jailed on another charge, but not charged with homicide for Carol's death. The event that triggered her murder will probably never be known.

The warning signs in these and other cases will be addressed in succeeding pages.

NUMBER ONE WARNING SIGN

Control is always the primary warning sign for murder. It is also the number one warning signal for violence. Murder is the final irrevocable step, the ultimate expression of men's control over women. For some men, the need for control is not satisfied until this irrevocable step is taken.

Because the common thread among these dangerous men is their unwavering, even obsessive, need for control over the women in their lives, they come from all walks of life. They may be unemployed or highly paid, a drinker or a non-drinker, with all types of family backgrounds, educational levels, and professions, including physicians, lawyers, and psychologists.

Control is the issue, but men who injure and kill are not "out of control" as is commonly assumed. They may be enraged or they may be cool and calculating, but they make a learned choice. No woman can "make them do it." Outside of the home, controlling men are generally law-abiding. Ninety percent have no prior criminal record. These men are dangerous only to their wives or female partners.

Wife murderers may not appear to be abusive men. Men who hold rigid, traditional views of sex roles and parenting have the

potential for endangering women because, as described, the patriarchal system places women under the control of men. Some men feel
that they have the right, even the obligation, to control their families. They feel that their male image depends on their ability to
dominate and control, and for this reason they often fail to recognize that they have been abusive. One-third of those who are violent
toward wives are also violent toward their children. The law often
reflects male privilege, including the view that the dead woman
must somehow have been at fault for what happened to her. This
has made it possible for dangerous situations to escalate.

Although women may no longer see themselves as "property,"
they often perceive their roles and needs as subordinate to those of
men. This can cloud their ability to recognize danger signs. Even
when the control is obsessive, many women view it as not far from
normal, whether they experience it as protective or uncomfortable
and demeaning. He sets the standards. Although women say that
they would never stay with an abusive man, large numbers of
women see nothing unusual in reporting, "He tells me I am always
late, but I'm trying to do better," or "Ralph says I spend too much
time visiting my mother."

Because control is the number one risk factor, sexist attitudes
become a risk factor. By themselves they do not lead to woman
abuse or woman murder. The "man in charge" role may work
when each partner is recognized as having complementary strengths
and deserving respect.

In addition to risks inherent in perceptions of traditional gender
roles, there are two other factors that add to women's risk. Both
involve men controlling women. One is the profile of the misogynist who has generally negative attitudes about women. The other is
"the man without a conscience." In either case, wives and lovers
become expendable.

MISOGYNY AND CONTROL

The misogynist, with his negative attitudes about women, typically keeps his wife continually off balance. She cannot please him,
at least not for long. She may be submissive to her husband or lover
in every possible way and yet experience ever-increasing amounts
of demeaning criticism. Or she may step out of her subservient role

to make a decision about her life, including that of leaving the relationship. In return she may receive a life-threatening response.

She may simply disagree with something he says and find herself threatened and intimidated. This man stands ever-ready to criticize and control. She can never be sure when he may attack, either verbally or physically. For no reason she may be able to fathom, he may go on a rampage that leaves her frightened, injured, or even dead.

Randy Vaughn represents the dark side of sexism and misogyny, although his behavior is better known than his attitudes. Randy's opinion is that he is in charge of his wife Brenda. He can victimize her at any time and in any way he chooses as an object of his aggression. In 1990 he was convicted of rape and of assault and battery. He was sentenced to 6 1/2 to 10 years in state prison. His repeated attacks on Brenda had resulted in several trips to the hospital emergency room. She divorced him, but he later persuaded her to move back into their apartment, a decision that is seldom safe.

In February, 1987, the family attended a party together. Because the time was getting late, Brenda suggested that they leave the party so she could put the children to bed. Well, how dare she embarrass him like that in front of his friends? At home he attacked her, fracturing a vertebra with his steel-toed boot. He ripped the phone from the wall to prevent her from calling the police. Later he demanded sex and, when she said no, he went ahead anyway. The next day she left with the children for a battered women's shelter.

Randy fled, and three years later, in 1990, he was brought back for trial. His lawyer said, "This is not your typical rape case . . . this is essentially a case involving essentially a man and his wife . . . this is not a normal rape. They were, for all intents and purposes, husband and wife. And God forbid if my wife decides to say 'no' to me and I want to go forward and she says 'no' and I do anyway. I will be standing right here . . . " The attorney went on to claim that this behavior is not uncommon in the disadvantaged community. "You fight. You make up. You fight again" (*Boston Globe*, Sept. 26, 1990). Randy's lawyer further stated his opinion that the violence in the home was not a "one-way street," neglecting to mention that Randy is 5'11", weighing 190 pounds, while Brenda is 5'3", and weighs 90 pounds.

In another case, a judge in the Bristol County, Massachusetts,

Probate and Family Court was reluctant to issue a restraining order against a Raynham, Massachusetts, man barring him from his home. The judge learned that the husband had come home drunk one night and demanded that his wife cook dinner for him. When she refused, the husband became violent. The tape recording of the proceedings documents the judge's response, "Not that you're required, but why didn't you have supper ready for him" (*Boston Globe*, Dec. 6, 1990, p. 34)? The judge's response reflects assumptions about men's entitlement and women's role that remain common—even to the point where the judge almost appears to understand why the husband might be provoked to beat her!

MISOGYNY AND EXTRAMARITAL AFFAIRS

Extramarital affairs occur among wife abusers and wife murderers and men who are not. They occur among men perceived as misogynists and those who are not. And affairs are prevalent among men whose attitudes toward women are ambivalent. Cultural support continues to exist for a certain degree of misogyny. The misogynist is given license to behave cruelly. His hunger for women's attention may be a never-ending quest even while accompanied by behavior that can only be destructive to the relationship. Whatever he does or says, his explanation will be she "wants" it or she "deserves" it.

Extramarital affairs do not usually change the misogynist's possessive hold on his wife. The more guilty he becomes (Forward and Torres, 1987), the more jealous he may become, erroneously assuming that she is seeking outside affairs just as he is. He seeks to place the guilt on her, thereby enabling him to feel less responsible for his own behavior.

His need to hold on to his woman is unusually strong, and if the woman attempts to leave, she may be in serious danger. His insatiable neediness makes him see her as his primary nurturer. His outside affairs help assure that he will never be left alone. Whether he is open or secretive about other women in his life, the misogynist's affairs serve to punish and humiliate his wife.

"YOU CAN'T TRUST A WOMAN":
THE ROOTS OF MISOGYNY

Researchers have attempted to profile the misogynist. Forward and Torres (1987) identify family background factors that may predispose one to misogyny, if not violent behavior or murder. Many of these are, to some degree, not uncommon.

Feminists decry offering up more reasons to blame mothers for societal problems, as though women have not heard enough about their supposed maternal shortcomings. In response, it may be said that women who have received inadequate nurturing and support from their families, and who receive little support from their mates, carry an extra burden when parenting. Women who have grown up uncertain about their own identity and lacking self-esteem have a more difficult time imparting values and empowering their offspring, whether their children are male or female.

Forward and Torres define abuse as any behavior designed to control and subjugate another human being through the use of fear, humiliation, and verbal and physical assaults. Whatever the choice of weapon, there is systematic persecution of one person by another (as opposed to occasional bad moods or expression of angry feelings). Psychological abuse includes implied threats, verbal attacks and unrelenting criticism, and shifting blame. The following behaviors are predictive of escalation to physical abuse: constant accusations, extreme jealousy, extreme possessiveness, continual watching (even spying), and overreaction to minor "infractions."

Woman's world, as a result, becomes narrowed. Control arenas include sexual selfishness, financial control (affluent men frequently leave their wives and children destitute), social life, restrictions on contact with her family, and jealousy of her relationship with her children. These men genuinely believe that their rage is due to their wives' deficiencies. "She" is the problem.

Forward and Torres list factors associated with the childhood backgrounds of misogynists. While the following list offers points to consider when selecting a mate, not all men with these backgrounds are misogynists, nor should these factors excuse men whose pattern is to "put women down."

1. He fears his father and has a strong dependence on his mother, thereby giving her the power to frustrate him. He may feel that he has to meet her needs to an excessive degree.

2. His father is a misogynist and his mother is helpless and submissive in her attempt to maintain the relationship at any cost. To get his father's approval, he must learn to control women. His father may be passive and unavailable to his son.

3. He feels suffocated by his mother's overwhelming needs and her role as a victim. He feels contempt that she cannot defend herself and feels controlled by her needs.

4. He believes that no woman can love him enough.

5. He believes that a man can never trust a woman.

6. If father is passive in relation to his dominating wife, blending into the background of family emotional life and retreating at the first sign of trouble, the male child learns that men cannot stand up to women.

The last factor, of course, excludes the healthy man who is gentle, quiet, soft-spoken, and emotionally intact — one not driven by the need "to stand up to women," to "prove his manhood."

The misogynist may see women as weak and childlike, especially if his mother could not protect him against a brutal father. He believes that he is entitled to have everything his own way, that women should rescue him from any discomfort. He is unwilling and unprepared to cope effectively with normal frustration levels.

Forward and Torres also describe the misogynist who has a cold and withholding mother, the opposite of the smothering mother who does not permit her child to learn how to deal with frustration. In this case, the man may see his wife as cold and treacherous, and anything less than her total involvement with his needs reactivates his earlier feelings of deprivation.

A man who finds it necessary to excessively deny his own emotional needs — to project an unrealistic image of male invulnerability — may use the unfortunate logic that his partner's dependency needs are also unacceptable, and he therefore he denies them. His extreme need for control over his partner often masquerades as an expression of love.

As other risk factors are recounted in succeeding pages, many of them will stem from (some) men's excessive need to maintain power over their wives or female partners. It would seem obvious that threats of physical attack, "I'll kill you," or "I'll kill her," need to be taken seriously. Sometimes they are not taken seriously.

Chapter Six

In Harm's Way

Women leading apparently normal lives are being threatened, intimidated, stabbed, shot, beaten, or killed in their homes at the hand of their mates. A particular characteristic of the dangerous man is spotlighted by experts. There is a marked discrepancy between the public image and the private behavior.

HE ISN'T WHAT HE SEEMS

Neighbors, bosses, and co-workers will not be attacked regardless of provocation. Only wives or girlfriends, possibly other family members, are in danger. From the perspective of the outside world, there appears to be no basis for assessing this man as a potential killer. Therefore, well-meant advice from family and friends to "patch things up" with this apparently ideal man may be all wrong, serving only to make her doubt what she sees and experiences. She may even see herself as the cause of the problem.

In the following case, probably no one will ever know what occurred during the marriage of George H. Gurney, Jr., 54, and his former wife, Miriam, 49 (*Boston Globe*, Dec. 3, 1990). Gurney was a well-respected man in his community. Miriam, now brain-injured, was formerly a New Hampshire schoolteacher and athlete. She now lies in a Massachusetts rehabilitation center, her life forever diminished, her testimony inadequate to convict her ex-husband. After two years and one million dollars of private health insurance, Miriam is now on Medicaid and about to lose her only remaining asset, her home.

After her divorce from George, Miriam had a secret affair. Her lover was a respected car salesman who was in a marriage that had lasted 29 years and produced four children. After a restaurant dinner, the two lovers returned to Miriam's home. Her ex-husband allegedly broke into the bedroom and shot Miriam in the head. Her lover died after being shot in the stomach, receiving 42 body blows, and being stabbed 17 times.

Gurney, who had just put down a condominium deposit, was held for 17 months without bail on charges of murder and attempted murder. After two trials and two hung juries, he was acquitted. Currently he is on leave from his job at the *Eagle-Tribune*, and Miriam knows that the man who (as she testified in court) tried to kill her is now a free man.

At home a man may yell at his wife or grab her by the arm to hurry her along. He gives orders. He tells her she doesn't know what she is talking about. He refuses to listen to her or he ignores her, giving her the silent treatment. He disappears for long periods of time without explanation. He disapproves of her friends and attempts to control what she does and where she goes. However, this is not the face he presents to the community.

Many dangerous men are well respected in the community and successful in their careers, often remarkably so. To neighbors and all those with whom they come in contact they present themselves as reasonable, quiet-spoken men who could never hurt anyone. "He was quiet and reserved, always willing to lend a hand." Sometimes he is described as affable and outgoing, always ready to be friendly. Only at home is his dark side revealed.

Who would suspect that a successful scientist who had obtained many grants for his well-known university would go home and kick his pregnant wife in the abdomen, causing miscarriage? His co-workers would never believe her story, even if she informed them. However, the man is dangerous, and her life remains at risk from her ex-husband, despite a court restraining order. If she informed his scientific colleagues about life at home, "They would think I was the crazy one and sympathize with him for being married to a woman who belongs in the psychiatric ward. Also, he would kill me for sure and probably get away with it." In no way does he fit the popular image of the easy-to-spot "brute." During the marriage, when police were called, he said something about his wife being "upset" over a "family fight."

Adams ("Identifying the Assaultive Husband in Court," *Boston Bar Journal*, 1989) describes the husbands, especially the professional men such as doctors, lawyers, psychologists, educators, or business executives, as they appear in court. The accused men are obviously well respected in their jobs and in their communities. Appearing in business suits, and accompanied by counsel, they are likely to present themselves as more credible than their agitated victims who may even be described as the aggressor in the "fight"! Even with no known physical or emotional abuse history, a marked discrepancy between the public image and the private person is considered to be a significant risk factor.

THE MAN WITHOUT A CONSCIENCE

He pretends to himself and lies to others as suits his purposes. His superficial charm and grace conceal a disturbing emptiness and lack of "character." Despite his pretense, no evidence can be detected that he feels any genuine empathy for others or remorse for his actions, whatever they may be. Psychologists and sociologists suggest that some men who murder wives or lovers may, from what can be learned about them, fall into this category. They are not viewed as mentally ill, even though they were first defined as psychopaths, then later as character-disordered personalities. In 1980, the American Psychiatric Association categorized them as having an antisocial personality disorder. This personality is described in *The Mask of Sanity* (Cleckley, 1982) and in other literature.

Commonly known as sociopaths, 3% percent of the male population falls into this category. As might be anticipated, both sexism and misogyny support the attitudes and actions of the sociopath. Like the sexists and misogynists, these men are also intent on controlling their wives and sexual partners. However, they do not present themselves as masters of the household or enraged misogynists who denigrate and demean women. Sociopaths attempt to play the social roles that society expects, even if the usual emotions are absent, and they will try to keep their image intact at home as well as in the outside world. However, the mask may slip. If this man is challenged, if his authority is flouted, the carefully hidden rage may emerge.

Women may not discover the dark side of these men for many reasons. Sometimes it takes years to detect that they are not what they seem. Women have been socialized to trust their mates and forgive them for whatever behavior does not seem sincere or caring. If his stories do not always "add up," wives see themselves as having few options except to deny contrary evidence and continue to try to make the relationship work. Whatever women do, these men do not change.

Sociopaths are described as arrogant, shameless, immoral, impulsive, anti-social, superficial, alert, self-assured, boastful, callous, remorseless, charming, and irresponsible (Cleckley, 1982). They are legally competent and none "hear voices" or display psychosis, but the results run the gamut from financial ruin to murder.

These "con artists" evade established definitions of sanity or insanity. They can manipulate some psychiatrists as well as other victims. Only one in one hundred spontaneously seeks help for the disorder, and neither the cause nor cure is known. As might be expected, many pass lie detector tests with ease. Despite good "intelligence" and superficial charm, they are unreliable and untruthful except when it serves their purposes. They may appear to show remorse to disarm the justice system, and they pretend to face consequences of their actions with fortitude, but, again, the purpose is to attain their own ends.

Sociopaths have a pathological egocentricity and incapacity for love, and their sex lives are impersonal. Their judgment is poor, insight is lacking, and they do not learn from experience. They may squander money, destroy relationships, or have brushes with the law, although they are unusually skillful at evading the consequences of their actions. Also observed is their failure to follow any life plan. They make promises they do not keep.

Early childhood educators describe attachment-disordered children who may later become sociopaths. For whatever reason, these children do not form normal attachments to parents and family, and the expected bonding and interpersonal relationships are impaired. Attachment-disordered children may have learned that adults cannot be trusted. The cause could be parents ill or impaired in some way, parents separated from children, prolonged hospitalizations, or many types of abuse. But this is a theory. [Sociopathic behavior can be described far more easily than its causes can be identified.]

The sociopath lacks respect for others and does not connect with them or love them. Furthermore, anger may erupt at any time in the form of rage or violence, and the sociopath will feel entitled to the hatred he exhibits. Some alleged or convicted murderers, such as Charles Stuart or Robert Marshall, do not present themselves as violent men. No one would expect them to shoot their wives or hire them to be shot. Why would Jeffrey McDonald or Steven Steinberg be charged with slashing their wives so brutally and repeatedly, far beyond the wounds necessary to kill them? Why would Kenneth Taylor murder his lovely young wife and drive off with his infant son to visit his parents, with his dead wife still in his car trunk? These men all seemed so much a part of comfortable, mainstream America.

Magid and McKelvey (1989) discuss children who cannot love, children who will not be loved. They grow up to be charmers, con artists, amoral entrepreneurs, thieves, pathological liars and, worst of all, killers. He notes that they are often the product of the most well-intentioned families. Among the characteristics of people who are "not what they seem" Magid and McKelvey list superficial attractiveness and friendliness with strangers, combined with lack of ability to give and receive affection. He, too, describes the "phoniness," lying, and, sometimes, stealing. In some sociopaths, he notes abnormalities in eye contact.

Levin (1991), an expert on sociopaths, emphasizes two other characteristics. First, the sociopath demands inordinate amounts of attention and admiration from others. Second, although he may flout morality and the law, he is well aware of right and wrong. He chooses to do what he does because he thinks he can get away with it. Also included in the category of sociopathic behavior may be extreme control problems, including hoarding goods or gorging on food. These individuals may be self-destructive in many ways as well as cruel to people or pets. A lack of long-term childhood friends is often part of the picture.

Sociopaths have a narcissistic personality, as described by psychologists, in which the individual is primarily concerned with his own image while presenting a mask of social grace. This person manipulates others to reflect what he wishes to believe about himself. If the mask is penetrated, the resulting rage can lead to violence. The narcissistic sociopath knows the "rules." He knows what other people feel even if he cannot experience the feelings himself. He knows how to look remorseful even if he is not. He is especially adept at shifting blame to others.

The suicide that sometimes follows a violent crime is described from the above explanation, as resulting not from remorse over what he has done but from his inability to tolerate exposure. He regrets that he did not commit the perfect crime that he had so meticulously planned. He is not sorry. Not even if he says he is.

Crime within the family shakes everyone's sense of trust. Who knows where the boundaries may be when couples experience the normal conflicts of life? Wife or partner murder is the ultimate betrayal as well as an event that pushes the control over one's spouse to the furthest limit.

No one has all of the facts for the following widely publicized cases described below. Experts have described these killers as character-disordered personalities. Learning about these cases reveals significant points to ponder about these "men without a conscience."

FAMOUS FACES, FAMOUS CASES

Charles Stuart

Why did Charles Stuart kill Carol Stuart, and exactly how did he do it? On the afternoon before his leap off Boston's high and majestic Mystic River Bridge, Charles spoke with his lawyer. Because the information was adjudged confidential attorney-client communication, it became unavailable. Some of the secrets, therefore, disappeared with his pre-dawn jump into the icy January waters of the Charles River. There could be no psychiatric examination or public testimony. However, there were many who knew him well. At least they thought they did.

Charles was born in Boston, just blocks from where his wife was shot on Mission Hill. He was the oldest child. His mother died during the birth of his sister, after which Charles's father married another woman with whom he had several more children. From all accounts, family life was happy and unremarkable and gave no hint of Carol's or Charles's eventual fate.

The Stuarts were both successful by all known standards. Charles's salary at the fur salon on fashionable Newbury Street near Boston Common was more than $100,000 per year. Carol was a lawyer, still at the beginning of her career. Charles and Carol had met while she worked at the Driftwood Restaurant near Boston Harbor to earn money for law school. Charles also worked at the restaurant. The two had known each other for years. After the murder, their smiling wedding picture (taken only four years before) appeared in major publications around the country, along with the romantic and touching letter he wrote to be read at her funeral.

Yet, on that misty October evening in 1989, Charles left the birthing class he had attended with his pregnant wife and drove in the opposite direction from their suburban home up into Mission Hill, where he later claimed they were robbed. His first story described a gunman entering the car and forcing him to drive to Mission Hill. According to another version, he was "lost." Still another story claimed that the robbery became a shooting because the "black man" saw the car phone and thought Charles was a cop!

After the shooting—Carol was shot in the head and Charles sustained a major abdominal wound—Charles's brother Matthew met him on Mission Hill by prearrangement. Matthew had apparently been told that this was an insurance scam. Matthew told his first lawyer that Charles handed him Carol's Gucci purse, her jewelry, and the gun. These were later retrieved from a river north of Boston where Matthew had tossed them. The gun was later found to have been stolen from Charles's employer, the Newbury Street fur salon.

Using the car phone, Charles called the dispatcher who recorded their conversation. Inexplicably, Charles continued to drive in directions that kept him in isolated areas and away from main streets where he might be more easily found. From the beginning the story was intriguing, but for more than three months Charles was not a suspect. Still, there were many unanswered questions, and the answers did not satisfy the voracious public appetite for understanding this story and bringing the killer to justice.

With Charles's leap from the bridge appearing to confirm his guilt, evidence began to accumulate about him and his possible role in his wife's death. In the hospital where Charles remained for several weeks while recovering from his gunshot wound, later alleged to be self-inflicted to divert suspicion, his behavior was noted. Some people suspected that something might be wrong with his story. He did not act as though he cared about Carol, he did not even mention her name. It was rumored that someone who visited him in the hospital called him a "bastard."

Carol died within hours of being admitted to the Brigham and Women's Hospital where she had attended a birthing class earlier that evening. It was recalled that she asked a question about cesarean surgery. The baby, Christopher, was delivered prematurely by cesarean section later that evening. He lived for 17 days.

Charles recovered faster than expected. When Carol's friend visited him at his parents' home after his hospital stay, she thought he might be in "bad shape," but was surprised at how cheerful he seemed. He even answered the door himself. At his barber's he had his grey sideburns touched up, and during a spritely conversation he appeared untouched by the deaths of his wife and premature baby.

Charles started spending Carol's $82,000 workplace life insurance check within days of receiving it. He filed other claims as well, some with double indemnity clauses in case of Carol's accidental death. Only eight days after leaving the hospital he purchased a pair of diamond earrings for just under $1,000. At another store he bought more jewelry, a $250 woman's brooch. Just days before his apparent suicide he purchased a 1990 Nissan Maxima car.

According to reports, Carol's father had not wanted his daughter to marry Charles, preferring another boyfriend instead, but Carol said she thought Charles loved her more. He wooed her with flowers and attention, and she was impressed.

Charles talked about having attended Brown University on a football scholarship and claimed he had dropped out because he hurt his knee. Brown has no football scholarships and the story was a lie. The truth was that he had been a mediocre student in vocational school where he had studied cooking and food service while earning money by working in a restaurant.

Charles always liked the finer things in life, and he was known for his taste in expensive clothes and furnishings. He aspired to a bigger house than the suburban split-level home he and Carol bought. His credit profile obtained after his death showed excessive credit obligations. Charles made many of the couple's household decisions. Carol willingly deferred to his judgment, although she expressed concern to her friends about their excessive spending.

Charles's interests included physical fitness and the couple often jogged together. It was important to Charles that he remain trim. They also entertained often and spent generous amounts of time with both families. Their friends suspected nothing amiss. Charles frequently returned to the working-class neighborhood in which he had grown up to play basketball with friends. He spent many evenings away from home, a known point of contention between him and Carol.

Apparently he also had at least one girlfriend during the marriage on whom he sought to shower attention. Telephone records showed that she called him at the hospital and visited him during his recuperation until she made the decision to end the contact. Some say Charles took the relationship more seriously than she did.

His talent for salesmanship had led to a swift rise at the fur salon, but, at 29, he aspired to more. Carol's salary as a young lawyer was still far less and she planned to quit her job, at least for a time, after the baby arrived. Marrying Carol had been a "step up" for Charles. She had helped him rise from his working-class background, but now she was becoming a hindrance to his dreams.

Carol trusted her husband so much that she remained untroubled by the number of life insurance policies he was taking out in her name. "We're becoming insurance-poor," she once said to a relative. "Chuck keeps taking out all these insurance policies on me." Still, it is doubtful that she knew the full extent of the insurance on her life. She also confided to her friends that she thought her husband would settle down and spend more time with her after they became parents.

The most common descriptive words used about Carol Stuart were that she was a happy person who always had positive things to say about people. She is described as very bright, but, in hindsight, also naive. But probably no more so than most.

It is said that Charles called his wife at work every day, often several times. If they had had an argument the night before, it was said that roses from Chuck would be delivered next day to Carol's office. Her friends were impressed, seeing this as evidence of an attentive husband.

While Charles was growing up, it is conjectured, he undoubtedly sat at the dinner table hearing his father, a Metropolitan Life insurance man, talk about the insurance business. Chuck may have thought of the idea then that big money could be obtained by eliminating someone. From the belongings he left behind it was evident that Charles loved murder stories. At the time no one understood the possible significance of a book he owned that told the story of Robert Marshall's attempt to collect insurance on his wife's life. It may have influenced Charles's apparent plans for disposing of his wife. One thing appears certain: Charles did not fall into the tangled web of hired killers that trapped Rob. Charles apparently did the job himself, but he did involve his brothers, and questions about their role remain.

Carol's murder was no sudden angry impulse. Charles planned her death in the methodical manner for which he was known. He apparently had no compunction about involving his younger brother in an "insurance scam" and, by diverting suspicion onto a black man in the disadvantaged community of Mission Hill, he was able to gain credibility for his story. Killing his wife immediately following the evening childbirth class they had both attended was a master stroke in diverting suspicion from himself, and it gained him enormous public sympathy. The final touch was provided by the grief-laden, loving letter from Charles to Carol that was read at Carol's funeral.

Charles's plans to eliminate his wife included asking advice(!) from at least two people: a friend and his firefighter/brother Michael. He asked about how "to get rid of" Carol, as both men later admitted to a grand jury. Evidence that Michael knew about the murder was provided on tape because Charles called his brother at the fire station where all calls are recorded. The two discussed telling their parents about (Charles's part in) the murder.

For whatever reasons, discussions about eliminating Carol took place without either man coming forward to warn or protect Carol. The friend turned down Charles's request, not taking it seriously, he said, and apparently thought no more about it. Charles simply and unemotionally informed his friend he wanted a restaurant instead of a baby. Carol planned to interrupt her career after the baby was born. Charles's big dreams and expensive tastes would not be facilitated by a stay-at-home wife and child. Charles needed capital to open a restaurant. About a month before Carol's murder, a staged break-in of their home by "intruders" was to incorporate an accidental shooting. The couple arrived home sooner than expected and the plot failed.

Questions continue about Charles's youngest brother Matthew's knowledge of the crime. Apparently he was not informed of the extent of the crime, he was told that it was only an insurance scam. Did Matthew notice his dead sister-in-law in the car when he took the evidence of the crime, including the gun, to drop into the river? Did Charles feel any guilt about involving his brother who carried the secret of Carol's murder for so many weeks? Did he really expect his brother, both brothers, to carry his secret forever? Would Matthew not question the fact that the purse Charles handed him contained a gun as well as jewelry? Matthew's first lawyer, the only lawyer who has spoken, revealed that Matthew's suspicions were first aroused that this was more than an insurance scam when he had to throw a gun as well as jewelry into the Dizzy River.

The lawyer claims that Matthew did not notice his dead sister-in-law in the seat beside Charles. Charles was in bad shape, too, having mistakenly shot himself in the abdomen instead of the foot.

Did Charles surmise that no one would question all that life insurance money? Nearly one million dollars total? Or the discrepancies in his story of what happened that night on Mission Hill? Did he think his jewelry purchases and immediate pursuit of another woman would raise no suspicions? Or was he supremely confident that his lies would hold up?

Investigators reportedly had their suspicions from the beginning, but had nothing substantive to refute Charles's story. Therefore, despite statistics pointing to husbands as prime suspects, they followed Charles's direction to focus the investigation on the Mission Hill community.

Except for Matthew's confession to his lawyer more than three months after the crime, made perhaps because the story was already out (Matthew's girlfriend's alarmed parents had apparently consulted their lawyer), Charles might well have committed the perfect crime. For the successful, handsome, smiling man, the game was up. Charles's betrayal of Carol shook the confidence of women everywhere.

Two Years Later: Carol Stuart's Parents Speak

Mr. and Mrs. DiMaiti broke their silence about their former son-in-law in interviews with P. J. Corkery (for a forthcoming book) reported in a series of headline articles in the *Boston Herald* (October 21-24, 1991). These articles confirmed and enhanced the image of Charles Stuart as a man displaying neither conscience nor remorse, a conspiring sociopath.

Chuck schemed to win Carol, and later, when her pregnancy interfered with his plans, in an eerily similar way he plotted her murder. In 1983 Carol had broken off her relationship with Charles Stuart saying that she needed more freedom, and the DiMaitis were relieved at her decision, recognizing that Carol's world was widening. Charles appeared to accept her decision. That summer Carol backpacked in Europe for six weeks with several women friends, deciding during the vacation trip to become a lawyer. Upon her return her parents met her at the Boston airport. They were surprised and dismayed to see Chuck disembark from the plane with their daughter. The apparently unemployed chef had flown to New York to meet her and accompany her back to Boston. She was carrying a large bouquet of roses. With his impressive gesture Chuck won Carol back.

Charles also had news of his new job with the furrier, neglecting to say that he had obtained it by lying about his background. The following Christmas he surprised Carol with still another grand gesture. Excitedly she called her parents on Christmas Eve to tell them Chuck had presented her with a silver box containing a leather wallet with the initials CAS for Carol Ann Stuart. Inside the wallet was a ring with a large diamond. Carol was engaged and happy. Her parents could only swallow their uneasiness and wish their beloved daughter well.

The two were married. Later the couple discussed buying a restaurant. If they had a baby the restaurant would have to wait. One Sunday, four years after the marriage, Carol informed Charles she would not accompany him to a restaurant conference. She thought she might be pregnant and the home pregnancy test she took that day confirmed it. Charles returned home to find his home decorated with pink and blue balloons, Carol's happy surprise for him. Although Charles concealed his true feelings, he was enraged as later attested by his friends. He felt betrayed. When Carol refused to have an abortion he began plotting. On the other hand, he purchased a generous supply of childbirth books, giving the impression of interest in impending parenthood.

Without success he attempted to involve his former classmate and his brother in a housebreak and murder scheme. He hatched a new plot to make his wife's death appear to be a racially-inspired killing that would divert suspicion from him, and even make him a hero. This event could be a real asset in his planned restaurant business. Two weeks before her murder, he took Carol for a Connecticut weekend to celebrate their anniversary.

During the pregnancy Carol remained close to her parents as always, seeing them for dinner once or twice a week and calling frequently. However, during the month before her death the Di-Maitis felt that Chuck seemed to be deliberately keeping Carol from them. On Sunday morning, the day before her death, she called to cancel the planned dinner at her parents' home saying that Chuck was tired. They would relax at home. Instead, Chuck got restless and the two spent the day at a shopping mall, then went to a movie and out to dinner. At 9 o'clock that evening Carol called her mother to say that the day had been like a "date." She had enjoyed herself. She also mentioned that Chuck was "out" helping a friend move using the fur company's van. Only months later did the DiMaitis realize that Charles spent that evening rehearsing their daughter's murder.

The DiMaitis recalled Charles's behavior after the murder, following his recovery from the supposed attack by the black man. They saw him as erratic, buoyant, and they felt he was not entirely "straight" with them. They wondered if their ways of showing grief were old-fashioned in today's world.

On Chuck's thirtieth birthday the DiMaitis called him, feeling that he might be lonely without Carol. In the background they heard sounds of a loud party with music. When Chuck finally picked up the phone he said he was too sick to talk.

Chuck suggested that Carol's parents meet him on Christmas Day at the cemetery at Carol's grave and set a time. The DiMaitis waited by the stone with Carol's picture on it, but Charles did not come. Later when they called him he said that his ride never showed up. The DiMaitis were sad. They could so easily have picked him up. Charles spent Christmas Day treating his family to a lavish restaurant dinner.

Not until the police knocked on their door late that January evening with their daughter's diamond ring did they know the truth. Charles was their daughter's murderer and he was dead.

Robert Marshall

Maria Marshall's murder was plotted with elaborate care. Yet, despite her husband's best-laid plans, he became a suspect the very night of the murder. It was not that he made any specific error or that there were any known prior warnings at that time. The police just did not believe his story.

Robert Marshall had long been a solid citizen of the upscale New Jersey town of Tom's River, and he was socially active with many friends. On the surface he seemed an unlikely suspect. As a successful insurance salesperson, making approximately $125,000 a year, he enthusiastically entered into the extravagant social life of the community, and every contact he made became a potential customer. During the past 20 years, Tom's River had grown and, with it, Rob's income. He eagerly approached new arrivals in town, welcoming them and orienting them to Tom's River.

Rob had a devoted and beautiful wife. In fact, Maria was so known for her blonde beauty that her husband often said "Isn't she gorgeous?" to friends and associates. And when he planned her murder he asked the hit men not to shoot her in the face. He said he didn't want her beauty marred. So, instead, she was shot in the back. The scenario went like clockwork.

Rob never appeared to understand why his explanations were not believed and why, in the end, his older sons could no longer support their father. Rob even seemed puzzled at their hurt bewilderment when, within weeks of their mother's death, he announced he would be bringing home a stepmother who would be "almost like Mom!"

On the night of the murder, Maria and Rob returned home from dinner at an expensive restaurant and an evening in Atlantic City. Maria was shot at 12:45 a.m. in a rest area off the New Jersey Garden State Parkway. The two gunshot wounds from the .45-calibre pistol were close together in the precise manner of professional executioners. Maria was found slumped face down on the seat, looking almost as though she were asleep. On the floor of the car was a single red rose.

Police officers knew right away that this was no panicky robbery attempt. Maria still wore her gold jewelry. Rob claimed that he had indeed been robbed and had lost several thousand dollars of casino winnings, but he was suspected by both police and almost everyone in Tom's River except his three sons.

There was no question that Rob was lying to the police. There would be as many more lies in the future as there had been in the past. Even Maria, his loyal and trusting wife, had recently found it necessary to seek answers to unsettling questions. In fact, it was these questions—the possible unmasking of Rob's apparent success—that, in his mind, apparently made it necessary that she die. Officers did not believe Rob's story that his rear tire felt "mushy" and that he drove into the deepest, darkest part of the rest area's pine woods to examine the tire with a flashlight. At least weekly he traveled this interstate highway to Atlantic City and he was well-acquainted with the road. The rest area was only two miles beyond the toll booth area, and it was just three miles before a Roy Rogers restaurant. Both were places where he could have stopped for help. Instead he turned into the Oyster Creek Picnic Area, made yet another turn, and drove his ivory Cadillac Eldorado almost as far from the highway as was possible to go before he finally parked. He never even tried to explain why he did that.

The clean, straight slash found in the tire's sidewall would have resulted in an immediate flat tire instead of the "mushy" tire Rob had described. (Later it would be revealed that the hit man almost forgot to slash the tire, and actually had to return to the murder scene to complete this part of the job!) Another aspect of the story did not ring true: Rob had never been known to change a tire in his life.

Rob had no explanation for why he got out of the Cadillac in those dark woods when the headlights of another car appeared behind him. His story was that as he knelt down by the tire he was hit on the head, and when he left the police station that night he did indeed sport five stitches on his forehead. It was unclear whether he also had a "bump" on his head as he later claimed. At the police station he appeared remarkably jaunty in manner as well as fashionably dressed in shined shoes, neatly pressed chino pants, and navy sport coat. He could not explain why his injuries were so minor during the alleged hold-up and why his wife in the car was killed. He was informed that he was considered a suspect and driven home. Rob fell asleep in the car.

At home, on 884 Crest Ridge Drive, his son Roby awakened at about 3 a.m. to find his father standing in the bedroom doorway with a priest beside him. His father was crying, and Roby noted his bloody shirt. Later he noted the stitches. In the afternoon, Rob traveled to his son Chris's college, to tell his son, "something terrible has happened."

Roby was surprised at how quickly his father became functional again, cheerful, fun to be with, making swift funeral arrangements. There was to be no viewing of the body. Maria was to be cremated immediately (although Rob never did pick up Maria's ashes from the funeral home where they remained for months). At the memorial reception in Maria's memory Rob played his role of genial host to the hilt.

From the first day after the crime Rob expressed more interest in who called on the telephone than in the well-being of his two older boys and his 13-year-old son. Rob wanted meticulous records kept of who called and the content of all messages that were received.

The two older sons could not help feeling that they had lost their father as well as their mother. In the past, Rob had always encouraged them in sports, attended their games, and taken the family on vacations. Rob had acted like a father. Was it all no more than a sham? The sons had not seen anything yet. All kinds of revelations and inconsistencies would emerge, and the ordered lives of the remaining Marshall family members would fall apart. In the months to come, nothing that happened would make sense.

Within 48 hours of the murder, on separate occasions, three people close to Rob had tried to point out to him the dangers of his situation: his lawyer friend, the husband of one of his sisters, and the bank loan officer. All spoke with Rob. For each question Rob had an answer that appeared adequate only to him. The bank loan officer did not buy Rob's story and told him so. He described Rob as arrogant, egocentric, and concerned only with status and appearances.

Rob continued to appear untroubled by the difficulties his story of the murder presented. With apparent candor Rob confided that he was having an affair with Felice (not her real name) and wanted this known. He appeared sincerely shaken when he was informed that his affair was not news, and that Maria had known about the affair, too. He was even more surprised when he learned that Maria had hired a private detective to find out what was going on. Rob then went on to say, inexplicably, that if he had known that she already knew, then "none of this would have happened."

In subsequent weeks he would deny the affair, complain that his wife had accused him of having an affair, and then say that plans were already made for Felice to divorce her husband and move to a place on the beach with Rob. Only a few days before the murder Rob had waxed eloquent at dinner with friends about how much he loved Maria. Talking with Rob was like jousting with air.

In their initial meeting after Maria's death, Rob's brother-in-law pointed out to Rob that there was a folder full of American Express receipts for motels and hotels that Maria had gathered the preceding spring in preparation for taxes. Rob's explanation was that these were dinners with clients. There were also puzzling telephone bills showing 40-50 calls per month to a school in a nearby town where Felice was vice principal. Love tapes to Felice were also stashed in the house. The trail was a mile wide.

Now the bereaved Rob suddenly became angry. He went on the attack. Maria had no right to go through his things and she had no business talking to his brother-in-law. The brother-in-law informed Rob that both he and Maria had planned to confront Rob the very week after she was killed.

Rob was told that Maria wanted desperately to save their marriage but was afraid to confront Rob alone. She feared his rage. In the past, whenever Maria had tried to discuss their problems with him, Rob was quick to lay the problems squarely on his wife. He even told Maria that she was losing her mind. He informed his wife that she was having a nervous breakdown and needed psychiatric help.

About the insurance money, Rob candidly admitted that, yes, he had taken out 1.5 million dollars' worth of life insurance on Maria; however, he explained, his business was selling insurance. How would it look if a man selling insurance did not insure his own wife? It was a wonderful sales tool. He explained that whenever he sold a policy to an executive or physician he always made a point of selling one on the client's wife also. The death of a spouse can have a big impact on the wage-earner. As for the amount, Rob saw nothing suspicious about having Maria insured for $1.5 million.

There were more revelations. Without Maria's knowledge, Rob had forged her signature on a $100,000 home equity loan application. Why the loan, and why the attempt at secrecy from his wife? Rob's glib answer was that he had a great opportunity to buy stock in a local cable television company, and that Maria was so unsophisticated in finance she would have become nervous if she had known. There were also other outstanding loans, and Maria had wondered where all the money was going. And well she might. At the trial it would be revealed that Rob was $300,000 in debt. He sold his boat to pay his lawyer. Rob continued to talk, complaining that the cause of their precarious financial situation was Maria's overspending. With one deft stroke he had shifted the financial problem to Maria!

As a final point, Rob informed his brother-in-law that he was a far too prominent citizen in the community to come under suspicion. He was confident that his reputation placed him beyond reproach.

Rob's brother-in-law and friends immediately advised him to hire a lawyer. The first legal advice he received was to stop seeing Felice, but within days Rob had contacted Felice, tearfully telling his lawyer that he couldn't live without Felice. During the three months following Maria's death, Rob would have affairs with at least three women.

Maria's murder in the Oyster Creek Picnic Area occurred in the early morning hours of September 7, 1984. With the greatest reluctance and trepidation, Maria had contacted a lawyer the preceding December. After her murder, he said that Maria very nearly changed her mind about revealing problems or even talking to him at all. She paid cash for the appointment. Unbeknownst to her friends, the preceding summer had been a nightmare for Maria who had wanted only to be a good mother to her boys and a supportive wife to Rob. The older boys observed that their mother occasionally seemed "edgy" and their father "remote," but there was hardly a ripple in the surface of their daily lives. In August the Marshall family went on a Michigan vacation.

Maria was the Tom's River East Swim Team Mother of the Year. She was described as her sons' best friend. As a sheltered doctor's daughter, Maria had never expected to be in the situation of seeing the family money disappear who-knows-where, discovering loans and debts, and knowing that her husband had been having an affair for at least a year while leaving an ongoing, obvious paper trail.

By the time summer arrived, Maria was increasingly concerned about Rob's activities. She was almost ready to consider divorce, even though her reason for seeking legal advice had been to understand and resolve the problems, whatever they were. She pulled back from divorce just before the family went on vacation, hoping that this almost unthinkable step would be unnecessary.

On July 23rd, immediately before the family vacation in Michigan, Maria wrote a note to her lawyer saying, "I'm holding my own, pray for me." Attached to her note were three Louisiana telephone numbers. These were later found to be the numbers of the hired killers.

As long ago as the preceding December, when Maria had first contacted a lawyer about her marital problems, Rob spoke to his woman friend Felice about "doing away with" Maria. Felice knew about the $100,000 loan, but only later did she learn the extent of his debts. At the time Rob said to her about Maria, "I wish she wasn't around. Do you know of anyone who could take care of it?" This, he said, would resolve his debt problem.

Rob Marshall spent that summer of the Michigan vacation busily planning Maria's murder. He was frantic because it took so long to get the job done. There were dozens of phone calls made between Tom's River and Shreveport, sometimes using pay phones.

The hit men made several trips to Atlantic City in addition to the numerous phone calls between Tom's River and Louisiana. More than once Rob gave them a sum of money, but, as they later testified, not always as much or as soon as had been agreed. There were numerous arguments about payment. Rob feared they would take his money without doing the "job."

At their very first meeting in June Rob actually wanted Maria killed that very night! He suggested to the hit men that the job be done in the parking lot of an expensive restaurant near the casino. The men toured the busy parking lot and thought Rob's plan made no sense at all.

One of the hit men who became involved in the scheme actually danced with Maria at a local party one evening. Another later saw the attractive blonde sitting quietly by herself at the Atlantic City casino where Rob gambled. She was sitting at the edge of the room. In her hand was a single rose. The man from Shreveport wondered briefly why a husband would dispose of a woman so beautiful.

On one trip from Louisiana Rob drove the men to the parking lot of the Roy Rogers restaurant on the Garden State Parkway. He informed them when he would have Maria at the restaurant parking lot. The hit men looked over the site and were appalled at the number of people in the area. There were even cops sitting in the restaurant. Again they went home.

Frantic calls came from Rob asking why the job was not done. The Michigan family vacation then required that the murder be postponed. However, on September 7th the "job" was finally completed. Rob had promised the killers that the remaining money he owed them would be found in his pants pocket, but after the shooting the killers discovered that Rob's pockets were empty.

The plan was carried out by dropping off one of the killers to wait in the rest area woods. This man would shoot Maria and wound Rob while the other man drove off to wait for Rob's car. After observing Rob's white Cadillac pass through the toll gate, this second man waited two minutes and then drove back to the picnic area to retrieve the man who had pulled the trigger.

Several days after Maria was killed, Rob's initial confidence in the success of his plan was shaken. Two men arrived at the house to speak with him. Rob called his son Roby downstairs to meet the visitors. Rob had just offered the detectives a drink, which they had refused, and he was offering to show them around the house when they presented him with the name of one of the hit men.

For the first time Rob appeared startled, then he immediately began lecturing the detectives on the appropriateness of the questioning, telling them to talk to his attorney. He announced he would have to terminate the interview. The lawyer whose name he gave them was no longer on the case.

On another occasion Roby took an urgent call for Rob from Louisiana. The son called his father who was staying at the beach with Felice. His father laughed off his concerns, saying the call had something to do with a basketball gambling debt. Roby had never heard his father mention basketball or known him to attend a game.

Later, Rob would give out the story that he hired the Louisiana men to follow Maria whom he suspected of having an affair. His sons knew this was also untrue, and their disbelief and pain intensified.

On September 26th, the townspeople of Tom's River learned that a hardware store clerk in Louisiana had been indicted on a conspiracy charge to kill Maria Marshall in New Jersey. Before long, two more men would be interrogated regarding the case.

Rob's next move, on September 27th, was to stage a fake suicide attempt in a motel room where he had spent time with Felice. He hoped to divert attention away from the investigation into what had happened to Maria. It was revealed that before the murder Rob had spent time with Felice in the Oyster Creek Picnic Area where Maria was killed, according to state troopers. More than once the troopers had chased them out.

Rob later said he had planned to commit suicide in the hotel room at 12:45 a.m., the hour that Maria had been killed, but he overslept. He dictated a rambling tape to Felice who had by then ended the relationship. He was trying to win her back. He also dictated a maudlin tape to his sons, but fell asleep in the middle of it. He had a bottle of pills, but had ingested none.

After the suicide attempt, Rob ordered his son to drive the 150-mile round trip each evening to the pleasant psychiatric hospital he was in to bring him his mail and messages. He told his son he did not suspect his wife of having had an affair. He insisted that the three boys come to visit him in the hospital. He desperately wanted his children on his side. He wanted their support in court. When one of his sons was later admitted to a psychiatric hospital, Rob showed no interest, nor did he ask any questions about the progress of the investigation into his wife's death. His attention was on overturning Felice's untenable rejection of him.

He was also of the opinion that her support would gain him sympathy and help his cause, especially when he realized the liaison was public knowledge. If the information was out, he might as well turn it to his advantage.

After leaving the hospital, Rob took a new girlfriend to Florida. He said he needed to get away from the stress. Once in Florida, his interest turned from the new woman in his life to the wife of his host. She and Rob then started an affair and the woman actually began to plan for a future with Rob. Rob said to his sons, from Florida, "You'll love her, boys. We'll buy a houseboat and we can all live down here."

Rob was arrested on December 19th. He continued to seek, and even expect, his sons' support. During the trial he called one of them three times in a futile attempt to get one son to lie under oath about his father's whereabouts on the day of the murder and thus discredit the testimony of one of the hit men.

In court Rob said, untruthfully, that his father-in-law, a physician, supported his innocence. Maria's father had never liked Rob and was deeply disappointed when his daughter insisted on marrying him. He finally gave permission if Rob graduated from college. Rob did graduate, but only because he persuaded one of his professors to change his grade from a D to a C. Maria's father was not in court, but upon hearing Rob's shocking statement the old doctor promptly had a heart attack.

From all accounts, from the many tapes he made, and from the testimony, it is difficult to find evidence of genuine communication with anyone (whether his lawyer or his sons) or realistic insight into his own horrifying situation.

Robert Marshall's story is told by McGinniss (1989). Rob appears to be trying to portray what he considers to be appropriate human responses, but he misses the mark. There are tears, the fake suicide attempt, and unrealistic hopes. He expends tireless energy in manipulating the truth and trying to escape the consequences of his crime. The concocted stories were glib, inconsistent, and unbelievable. His actions after the murder enmeshed him ever more deeply. For example, he was still maneuvering to buy more life insurance on his wife the very week that she was killed. And, during the trial, the wife of one of the accused hit men even stayed briefly in Rob's house!

The home movies of Christmases past and of all those family vacations remained, but this was a man who, largely because of his gambling and uncontrolled spending, could make plans to "do away with" his partner of 20 years and the mother of his sons. After the murder, his mask of the model husband and father completely fell away. How could the mask apparently stay in place as long as it did? One can only conjecture, but for the sake of women everywhere it is important to consider some likely answers to this important question.

Rob appeared as an engaging, lively, successful member of his social set. At the trial his lawyer pointed out, in his defense, that his client had no criminal record and had been a model citizen. His sons had seen him as an involved and loving father. One son continued to believe in Rob's innocence. Maria had lived with Rob for 19 years before seeking help, and it is doubtful that she suspected Rob wanted her dead, or that he could, or would, conspire to cause her death.

Maria was an asset to Rob. She was ornamental, bright, loyal, and supportive. She produced three successful and handsome sons. Rob had his fantasy of the ideal, all-American family; a beautiful, well-kept home; and a lively social life that accompanied the assets of a successful family. It was a big change from the shabby apartments where he spent his boyhood as the son of an alcoholic father.

Maria was the stabilizing force for the family. She made sure that everyone's needs were attended to and she held it all together. If

Rob lacked his wife's sense of integrity and responsibility, these deficiencies would not be obvious, largely because Maria fulfilled her responsibilities so well.

What cracked the facade? It was not Felice who, although married, was known to have had relationships with a number of men. Her flamboyance satisfied Rob's thrill-seeking nature, but marriage or a committed, loving, long-standing relationship with her was probably not in the cards. It was his desire and need for money, and lots of it, to feed his voracious need to gamble and to spend, whether or not women were involved. He sought a free-wheeling lifestyle with no thought of the consequences.

He could not abide the thought of Maria divorcing him, and he did not want the resultant financial cost and damage to his reputation. Any way a divorce was done it would be costly and unpleasant. A divorce was not something he wanted or needed.

It is conjectured that Maria was in jeopardy because she was asking too many questions about his activities. It would be awkward if his family learned that he had spent all the family money and more. How long could he lie about his debts? How much simpler it would be if Maria could simply disappear, her life exchanged for the $1.5 million dollars that would rescue him from debt.

The court verdict was guilty.

Kenneth Taylor

Like Charles Stuart and Robert Marshall, Kenneth Taylor presented himself as personable, good-looking and successful—the sort of man to whom women were easily attracted. He had no police record and nothing in his manner suggested that he was capable of violence. Certainly he did not appear to be the homicidal maniac described by one of the psychiatrists who later examined him.

Teresa's life was not "traded in" for a major insurance pay-off as in the cases of Charles Stuart and Robert Marshall. It was true that the $100,000 insurance policy may have played a minor role in the subsequent vicious custody battle for Teresa and Kenneth's five-month-old infant son, but chances are the custody battle would have occurred in any case.

Nevertheless, from what can be learned about the three murders, similarities appear in the personalities of the three men: manipulating others and playing society's roles without the emotions that usually accompany interpersonal relationships. It was said about Ken that he never really laid all his cards on the table.

Ken was immediately suspected of being Teresa's killer, even before her body was found. He had no police record, but there was just something about this case. Early in the investigation Ken confessed because he had more to gain by explaining why he killed her, attempting to divert attention from himself as the murderer, than by trying to refute the damaging evidence of the bloody slaughter. Ken tried to say it was her fault. She started it. If Teresa had not swung that 30-pound weight-lifting bar at him, none of this would have happened. He acted in self-defense. Later he added other embellishments to his story of why he had to do what he did — kill his wife.

Ken's behavior after Teresa's disappearance was odd. If he had told a believable story and exhibited anything resembling the expected emotions under the circumstances, it is possible that he might have gotten away with the crime.

The question was why? How could he commit this act against his beautiful and loving wife? No problems in the marriage were apparent to anyone and, even if there were, could anything explain what happened? What could have provoked an apparently reasonable and intelligent man to commit a crime that appeared so senseless and self-destructive? It could put him behind bars. Even if he were not caught, what would he gain?

Ken seemed to create his own reality; he was glib and ever-ready with explanations, including why he killed his wife. If there was any apparent remorse, it was clear that it was displayed only to help him win his case. He seemed confident that his explanations would be accepted. Teresa had brought it on herself. His wife, he claimed, provoked him to kill her. His defense was that another man in his circumstances would have done exactly as he did. Ken's parents fully agreed with their son and continued to support his stance during the trial and afterward. What about his previous wife whom he unsuccessfully tried to kill? Did she also drive him to violence? This question was never asked in court because the story of his attack on the second wife was excluded from the trial.

After his conviction and a life sentence he said, "I'd always looked forward to being a jolly grandfather with a house or yard full of rowdy grandsons and cute little tomboys or dainty granddaughters.'' Was this man for real? There was little in Ken's life story that could lead anyone to suspect that this was his goal!

Finding himself in prison, the former dentist right away began busily began planning his jailbreak. With unshakable optimism Ken made at least three shrewd but unsuccessful escape attempts. He was still acting as though he could escape the consequences of his actions.

Peter Maas (1990) raises many warning flags during the telling of Ken's life story. On the surface, the Taylors appeared as a typical upstanding family in a small midwestern town. His mother was a den mother for Cub Scouts. His father coached school sports in his spare time and his mother attended to cheer the games. According to Ken, his parents were "strict but not tyrants."

The Taylors attended the local church, and Ken often told the story that his family was once on the cover of the annual church calendar. There was only one problem with the story: there was no family photo and there was no church calendar. Ken lied even when there was no apparent reason, but he always sought to enhance his own image.

Ken's peers described him as affable and easygoing, popular enough to be elected vice president of the student council during his senior year. The one negative note was their description of him as a teenager tying his sister to a chair in front of other teenagers and painting her hair green. They said Ken was enraged because his sister tattled to their mother.

During his senior year in high school his parents moved from Ohio to an Indiana town, leaving Ken behind to finish his senior year. He stayed with a friend, getting his first taste of freedom with no curfew and the use of a car known as the "sexmobile."

In college he cultivated an "aw shucks" manner because, he said, it seemed to attract girls. He was blonde, over six feet tall, and weighed 180 pounds. To keep in shape he lifted weights. During college his first serious girlfriend rejected him and he vowed to friends that this would never happen to him again. At age 20, during his junior year of college, he eloped with Emily (not her real name). He informed his mother, saying, "I wanted to marry some-one just like you, Mom."

To his family's pleasure and surprise, Ken announced that he would become a doctor (possibly to attract some of the attention away from his brother's sports success). Because Ken's grades were not good enough for medical school, Ken fabricated a story he told to almost anyone who would listen, especially women. He was fond of describing the sad scene when, as a hospital orderly, he was handed a bundle which turned out, he said, to be a dead baby. He thought about what it would be like to have to face distraught parents with the news of their child's death. To avoid this possibility, he decided instead to become a dentist. The dead baby story was, of course, just another fabrication, but he was able to wangle a Naval dental scholarship. In fact, he gave such a polished performance that the interviewer called him "an outstanding officer candidate."

Emily was teaching in Ohio, and because he saw her only on weekends, Ken had plenty of free time to seek other companion-ship. When Emily found a stash of drugs in their apartment closet, Ken told her he was "holding it for a friend." To others he said, "you got the drugs, you get the girls."

Emily became pregnant during Ken's third year of dental school. At first he seemed pleased, but he then became sullen. Emily finally asked if he cared about the baby. His response to his shocked wife was, "It's not my kid. You've been fucking around." Just days before the baby's arrival, without warning, Ken packed his things and walked out of their tiny apartment. When Emily returned home on that June day there was not even a note. She never saw Ken again. Later, when Emily remarried, she wrote Ken to ask his per-mission for her new husband to adopt the boy. Ken refused. Ken's mother thought Emily had brought her troubles on herself. Emily, she complained, wouldn't even watch Kenny play softball.

While working nights as a desk clerk near the airport, Ken met a sophisticated, long-legged flight attendant described by Ken as a "knock-out." Could he explain his past with enough credibility to entice his new girlfriend to start a relationship? Well, yes, of course he could.

At first the new woman did not know Ken was married. He then said he was getting a divorce and that "Emily tricked him by getting pregnant.'' (Later, when his friend from college telephoned, Ken never even asked how Emily was.) When the new girlfriend discovered Ken's heavy drug use, his response was that he needed a woman like her to help him quit. They moved in together, and Marilyn (not her real name) became his second wife.

Ken's dental education was going badly, but he confidently approached the school to request that he be given an extra year to graduate. He informed the school that he needed the time because of "family problems." The request was granted.

It was just five years after walking out on Emily that Ken tried to kill Marilyn. He explained later that he did it because he "was in a bind." After the attack, Marilyn decided not to file a formal complaint, and she remained in the marriage. The relationship between the two was never completely severed, even during Ken's third marriage. Ken was very persuasive.

During Ken's marriage to Marilyn a number of events occurred, and many of them, although not uncommon, added up to a potentially dangerous situation for Marilyn. She was exposed to ongoing emotional pain throughout the marriage, although there may have been "good" times, too. Certainly, at least in retrospect, she could not trust much of what he said or did.

Ken pretended to enjoy nearby New York cultural life, but he was restless. He skipped graduation and the two moved to Indiana for a time, to be away from "dopers." Marilyn did not complain about the move. Once there, Ken used fewer drugs but more alcohol. Although the couple lived only half an hour away from Ken's parents, Marilyn never met them. On the phone, Ken's mother said to her, "You could at least have waited until he was divorced before you moved in with him."

Ken filed a false crime report. After a softball game he ran his car into a utility pole and drove the dented car home. Later he abandoned the car on a country lane and then reported it as stolen to police. However, neighbors who had seen the car at the apartment complex after the accident refuted his claim. When caught in the obvious lie, Ken claimed that he told the falsehood because he feared his wife's anger. He begged her forgiveness.

There were many women in Ken's life and he claimed that "they were all the same." On one occasion Marilyn found a note from a woman under their door, and Ken lied saying that it was meant for a man living down the hall. Marilyn was mortified when she discovered she had a case of sexually-transmitted "crabs," but Ken denied responsibility. He then accused his wife of having extramarital escapades.

Ken moved out of the apartment. His explanation was that his wife was trying to control him. At about this time Marilyn's father was diagnosed with throat cancer. Marilyn, distraught, turned to her husband for comfort that he pretended to provide. She then moved into his new living quarters and their relationship resumed.

Marilyn became pregnant. When she accused Ken of stealing $300 she had saved for baby clothes, he swung his fist at her. She ducked and his fist hit the refrigerator with such force that he broke his hand. His hand was placed in a cast. On April 16, 1978, with his hand still in the cast, Ken offered his pregnant wife a cup of hot chocolate. Marilyn was touched by his solicitude. She noted that the drink that Ken brought into the bedroom had a strange odor. "Sleep well," he said. She was so tired that she fell asleep without drinking the hot chocolate. Her life was saved, for the moment.

Near midnight, several hours later, Marilyn awakened to sense a shadowy presence in the bedroom. Her husband came over to her side of the bed and sat down. At first she thought he might be planning to apologize for his earlier behavior. She felt his arm hard on her chest. Something rough was pressed against her mouth and nose. She smelled the same fumes that she had noticed in the hot chocolate, but they were much stronger. She tried not to breathe. She managed to break free long enough to beg him not to kill her. She promised to do anything he wanted. Still he said nothing.

Ken had wrapped a sponge soaked in chloroform in a kitchen towel. As a dentist, chloroform was a substance to which he had access. Chloroform kills in less than five minutes and is not detectable in an autopsy. During the struggle, the towel slipped away, leaving the sponge directly against her face. Marilyn could not believe that she was about to die at the hands of her own husband in her own bedroom, and she did not even know why. She thought of her father dying of throat cancer and managed to roll onto the floor. Ken was right on top of her. She managed to twist onto her stomach and felt the cast on his broken hand press against the back of her neck. Suddenly Ken stood up.

The Naval chaplain drove Ken and Marilyn to the hospital. Ken was scheduled to see the psychiatrist. Marilyn's face was almost unrecognizable; it was puffy and raw from the chloroform. Because she did not die, the attack could be described as a "domestic battering" incident except that chloroform was used. However, he had stopped short of killing her. Much was made of his restraint.

Ken did not deny that he tried to do away with his wife. He blamed it on drugs. Also, he said, he was in a bind because he feared his parents' reaction to another broken marriage.

As for Marilyn, she remembered wonderful moments with Ken. She thought about his career. Did she want to destroy his life because of one incident? The psychiatrist who first saw Ken gave Marilyn his opinion that Ken was a homicidal maniac. The second psychiatrist, the first one's superior, had a different opinion and essentially seemed to whitewash the whole unhappy incident. He seemed protective of Ken, while placing a burden on Ken's wife. The psychiatrist informed Marilyn that her husband was not dependent on drugs, that there was no evidence of psychosis. He said that Ken had difficulty in dealing directly with his emotions. His words to Marilyn were that Ken experienced a growing lack of respect and appreciation from his wife, and that Ken had feelings of abandonment due to Marilyn's father's illness. The psychiatrist informed her that Ken had agreed to counseling and the psychiatrist urged Marilyn to cooperate!

If Marilyn had her doubts, they were not validated by the professional evaluation. She may have wondered about her own ability to judge the seriousness of her experience of being chloroformed! Her husband had admitted he tried to kill her, but she had been reassured. After the psychiatrist's lecture, Marilyn decided not to file a formal complaint. The result was that there was no media coverage, and there could be no public knowledge of the murder attempt. The intriguing story circulated and the result was that still more women flocked to Ken.

Ken explained to his parents that he had lashed out physically because of too much coffee and pills. These were consumed as a result of marital tensions caused by the way Marilyn had been treating him. He explained that he was now in therapy to "build his self-esteem." The way things were going he would need a $10,000 loan from his parents to retain a lawyer. (Ken never repaid the loan.)

Marilyn gave birth to the baby. Ken played the doting father and the supportive son-in-law for Marilyn's father's last days. The family moved to New York where Ken was to run a newly established dental clinic. There were more women in Ken's life, and Marilyn blamed herself. She felt guilty because somehow she was never really comfortable with Ken after the chloroform attack!

In September, 1980, in the Brooklyn dental clinic, Ken met his third wife, Teresa Benigno. Teresa would never learn that Ken had been married to Emily, his first wife. She would know of his marriage to Marilyn, but would never know about the murder attempt. Furthermore, when Teresa's mother later asked Marilyn whether Ken was capable of violence, Marilyn saw no need to share anything with the Benignos. Whatever had gone wrong in her marriage to Ken, she felt no need to protect Teresa. Ken still pulled the strings that controlled Marilyn's information about Teresa. The result was that Marilyn's view of the Benigno family was as false as Ken cared to make it. For all of the above reasons, Ken could start a new relationship with his reputation untarnished.

Teresa was a dental hygienist in the dental office, and Ken was immediately attracted to her. Teresa was warm, happy, and eager to learn and do her best. She had beauty, and Ken found her blue eyes and classic figure especially appealing. This was a woman he wanted and he set his sights on impressing her.

Ken courted her so successfully that in spite of any doubts her family had there was little they could say. He directed his charm to the Benignos, a close-knit Italian family on Staten Island, New York. Somehow her parents remained vaguely uneasy, although they could identify nothing specific. Teresa's grandfather showed obvious displeasure with the suave and glib Ken, but Teresa was in love with Ken. Although her attachment to her family was so strong she had chosen not to go away to college, she wanted to marry Ken. The family gave the couple their full support.

Teresa's father had written in her high school yearbook that the man she would marry would make the ultimate difference in the outcome of her life. Her father hoped that she would marry someone her equal in both intelligence and maturity. He wrote that that man must never be her master, dictating the terms of her security through force or fear. He concluded his message by saying that marriage endures only with mutual love and respect for one another.

Ken and Teresa began their affair. In March of 1981 Ken brought Teresa's mother a birthday bouquet and thanked her for bringing such a beautiful daughter into the world. However, Teresa's friends saw Ken as remote, disinterested, smug, and taking little part in their conversations. When Teresa became pregnant, Ken insisted that she have an abortion, which she did. Apparently, he could not resist saying to her "Is it mine?"

Ken had not changed. He still behaved as "a man without a conscience," and continued to mislead and lie. Teresa planned a birthday celebration for him that included her gift of an expensive stereo system. The evening passed. Ken never showed or called. Later, he made amends by saying his divorce from Marilyn was now imminent. He admitted that he had been in Pittsburgh visiting his daughter and expediting the divorce from Marilyn. Teresa forgave him, especially because there was progress in the divorce action. There was no way she could have known what he was really doing.

The true story was that, yes, he had been in Pittsburgh—in bed with Marilyn. While in Pittsburgh he asked Marilyn to drop the divorce proceedings. Teresa, he complained, was "immature." While at Marilyn's he mowed the lawn and acted in the manner of what he believed to be the model husband. He needed sex, he claimed, to boost his low self-esteem. He was pleased and impressed that Marilyn had new breast implants, and she had done it for him. Apparently she was jealous of Teresa and wanted him back, and that was good news.

The facts were that if Ken divorced Marilyn to marry Teresa he estimated that the divorce would cost him $500 per week. Marilyn would get the house. It was true that she had supplied most of the down payment, but he was irked at the thought of Marilyn getting the house.

Back in New York, Ken had yet another story for Teresa. Marilyn, he announced, was threatening to blackmail him for more money. She had photos of Teresa naked on a beach and she was threatening to send them to Teresa's parents. The reason Teresa had not seen them was that he just couldn't bear to show them to her, he said. Teresa told him that she had never been nude on a beach in her life. Ken took another tack, saying that they had Teresa's head superimposed on someone else's body, but he would not cave in to Marilyn no matter what she did. Teresa was distraught and confused, and when she spoke to a friend, her dismayed friend's opinion was that Ken was playing "mind games" with Teresa.

Despite Ken's efforts to halt the divorce from Marilyn, she made the decision to divorce Ken, clearing the way for his third marriage. On July 10, 1983, Ken and Teresa were married. Of the 150 wedding guests, none were friends of Ken. Ken couldn't come up with a guest list. Even his brother couldn't come. The reason the family gave was that his brother had a serious drug problem (so serious that he had failed his college courses).

The couple honeymooned in Acapulco. Shortly before Ken and Teresa were scheduled to return to New York, the Benignos called the hotel, only to find that the couple had checked out and left no forwarding address.

Marilyn had not been told that Ken was getting married, only that he was going on a short vacation. She knew nothing about the wedding. When he didn't show up at her place as promised, Marilyn called the flabbergasted Benignos.

Just days after the wedding, Teresa was viciously attacked in their honeymoon hotel room. She was left barely alive and lying in a pool of her own blood. Her throat was slashed and her face was a purplish mass. One eye was open, but it was only a slit in her puffy face. Her lips were black and cracked, and all that remained of her front teeth were jagged fragments. Glass was removed from her eye. Stitches were required in her eyelid as well as her face and neck.

Ken claimed that they had been attacked in their hotel room. After the intruders left, he had gone out on the balcony. When he returned he saw Teresa slumped on the floor in the corner of the room unconscious. Ken had no visible injuries except for a few scratches.

Ken was placed in a Mexican jail but was soon released, complaining mightily about conditions in Mexican prisons. It would later be noted that the honeymoon was financed using Teresa's credit card. Teresa's hospital bill was financed by her American Express credit card. Ken's credit cards had all been canceled, and he owed Sears $612.

Teresa maintained that she did not know who had attacked her. The reasons can only be conjectured: fear of Ken, the humiliation, his assurances that it was all a big mistake. Possibly there was retrograde amnesia, meaning that when she became unconscious she lost memory of the preceding moments. Perhaps she really did not know exactly what had occurred prior to the assault and was unconscious during much of the attack. She never confided in anyone.

After being released from jail, Ken remained at Teresa's side. He had obtained money from a fellow guest at the hotel, a person who later came forward to be a prosecution witness at Ken's murder trial. Of course, Ken had a story. He and Teresa had been attacked in their hotel room and his temporary imprisonment was part of an outrageous Mexican shakedown.

In the hospital, a nurse heard Teresa cry out. She entered the room to find Teresa stumbling back against a wall. When she asked Teresa what was wrong, Ken answered for his wife, saying that Teresa had temporarily lost her balance. Teresa remained silent.

On the plane trip home Ken dosed Teresa heavily with Valium, for pain, he said. Later, Ken pressed large amounts of codeine and other medications on her, also for pain, as he explained to her and to others. He said it was all part of her recovery from the hotel room attack.

Ken quit his job with the dental center to be with Teresa, according to his story. He announced that he would launch his own practice. The truth was that there was at least $5,000, maybe $10,000, missing from the dental center. Rather than press charges against Ken, others in the practice wanted him to resign. Ken proudly showed his letter of resignation from the dental center to the Benignos. How he expected to open a practice with no credit was never discussed.

Teresa's mother confronted Ken. She informed him that the hospital psychiatrist's opinion of the attack was that Teresa's husband had done it. Ken's indignant response was what did the psychiatrist know? Why doesn't anyone believe Teresa? At dinner with the

Benignos he was bland and cool, showed no irritation or temper, and acted as though his own survival from the attack was a miracle. Still uneasy about Ken, Teresa's mother called Marilyn to ask if Ken was a wife-beater. The short response was, "He never beat me."

Three days after the return from Acapulco Ken was again mowing Marilyn's lawn and telling her that the muggers in the hotel room had been in cahoots with the cops to make it look as though the husband had done it. Ken went on to say it was Marilyn's fault that he had married again. If only she had postponed the divorce; instead she had rejected him and Teresa was relentless in her pursuit of him. He assured Marilyn that his marriage to Teresa would not last.

Ken's parents never came to visit Teresa either in the hospital or later at home. They were assured that their son was fine.

The marriage of Teresa and Ken continued its course. Whatever the doubts, no one person knew the whole story on Ken, including Teresa. For those who knew her, only the inexplicable and mysterious Acapulco attack could elicit a clear alarm signal regarding her safety. Teresa had somehow accepted that unfortunate episode, perhaps putting it behind her as an isolated incident that occurred under unusual stress. It would never happen again. She loved Ken and her goal was a successful marriage. She remained upbeat.

Even if Teresa and her family had learned about the earlier attack on Marilyn, Ken would undoubtedly have patched together an explanation for them, as he did for his parents. Through manipulation, Ken controlled "his" women and all with whom he came in contact. This would be evident once again with regard to his infant son. From behind prison bars he masterminded the vicious and tenacious custody battle.

Interrupting the marriage would have been a difficult step to take. If his mask had been penetrated and Teresa had initiated an attempt to leave him, it is possible she would have found herself in the same terrible danger she faced by continuing on in the marriage as his loving wife. In retrospect, the dark clouds swirling around Ken continued to accumulate unchecked. No single event appeared sufficiently ominous to raise serious questions about the marriage. And it is unlikely that either Teresa or anyone else saw the possibility of wife murder.

When Teresa became pregnant, Ken appeared excited and proud. However, on a trip to Pittsburgh he assured Marilyn that she was really his true love, but now that Teresa was pregnant what could he do? Marilyn was sympathetic to his plight.

To Teresa and her family, Ken seemed proud of his approaching fatherhood, yet there was another disturbing note. Later, Teresa confided worriedly to her cousin that Ken had wanted her to get an abortion for this pregnancy, too, as she had done before the marriage. This time she had refused.

During discussions among friends and family after Teresa's death it was only too clear how much was unreal. The stories Ken told to various people did not jibe. The vague uneasiness felt by many during Teresa and Ken's marriage was more significant than anyone at the time could have realized.

When three couples, including Teresa and Ken, vacationed at a resort they had adjoining rooms. Teresa appeared anxious and insisted on the middle room, saying, "If something happens I want everyone to hear it." She offered no further explanation and the vacation was otherwise uneventful.

During the pregnancy, Ken made a show of pampering Teresa. He was so successful that her friends made an example of him to their own husbands. However, the husband of one of Teresa's friends watched Ken fly into an incredible rage when he hooked a shot on the golf course. Ken flung the iron 30 to 40 yards, it was said, and began kicking, cursing, screaming and stomping. When they returned home from the golf game, Ken picked up Teresa's cat and slammed it twice into the garage wall, saying angrily, "the goddam, fucking cat."

Teresa confided to her cousin that Ken smoked pot and did coke to get through his work day. She explained that there was so much pressure at work, so much tedium, and problems with overhead expenses and Medicaid. She admitted that in the past she had occasionally done coke with Ken, but now that she was pregnant she was no longer willing to do drugs with her husband. She also hinted worriedly about Ken's sex practices and wondered if other husbands had similar needs from their wives.

When premature labor threatened during the last weeks of her pregnancy, Teresa was ordered to remain in bed. After a labor described as difficult, she gave birth to a son. The day the baby was born Ken wrote a moving letter to his wife saying that on that day she had shared with him the greatest gift of all, the gift of life. The proud father act was displayed to the fullest. No one can know what was really in his mind, how much of a charade his act might have been.

Following the arrival of their first grandchild, Ken's parents arrived from Indiana. Their visit, from all accounts, was not a happy time for Teresa. Her mother-in-law was critical and later told others the unbelievable story that the Benigno family did not get along. She even claimed, untruthfully, that Teresa had left home after high school because of family conflicts. During the visit, Ken told Teresa, and everyone else, that his mother had to be in their home because Teresa needed his mother's experienced guidance on newborn care.

Although Ken's mother allowed the men in the family to eat meat, she herself would not eat meat, nor allow Teresa to do so, even though Teresa was a nursing mother. Teresa complained to friends that she was being starved, but in the home she kept the peace. The meals her mother-in-law provided were so scanty that the breast-feeding Teresa could no longer supply enough milk for the baby. The baby was put on formula and Ken's mother was glad to see that the baby was now gaining weight.

It was Teresa who supplied the money for the down payment on their suburban New Jersey house, as she had for their Acapulco honeymoon. Ken took out a life insurance policy on Teresa, explaining that now that she was a mother, insurance protection was important for their son. The decision seemed reasonable and responsible to Teresa.

For Marilyn, Ken had another story. He complained that Teresa was freaking out on cocaine, that she was forging his name on codeine prescriptions. In truth it was Ken who was writing prescriptions and putting his wife's name on them. He even told Marilyn that Teresa was freaking out so much that he feared for the baby's safety. He said he wanted to leave Teresa to return to "his family," meaning Marilyn and their daughter. He wanted to get custody of the new baby. He admitted to Marilyn that to accomplish this he was keeping precise records on Teresa's "drug abuse."

The usually cheerful Teresa was becoming noticeably less so, and her sister therefore persuaded her to go into the city for a day of shopping. At the end of the afternoon her sister was surprised at how important it was to Teresa that she get home on time. Teresa looked pale and even frightened at the possibility of being late. Her sister was impressed with Teresa's dedication to wifely responsibilities and vowed that from now on she would be a better wife to her own husband.

Several disturbing events occurred during the months following her baby's birth. Teresa had looked forward to being home with her baby. To her intense disappointment, Ken insisted that she return to work shortly after the baby was born. It was with great reluctance that she dropped her baby off at her mother's each morning. She had no choice.

Then, without explanation, Ken disappeared for a couple of days. Upon his return he explained that he was desperate to see his daughter in Pittsburgh, and he begged Teresa's forgiveness. She forgave him.

Teresa had thought her earrings had been stolen in Acapulco. One evening when guests were in the house she idly opened Ken's briefcase and expressed bewilderment at seeing her earrings. Ken said, no, this was a different pair. To her friends' surprise, Teresa asked no questions. Her only response was an acquiescent "okay."

Teresa's end was near. Her baby was now five months old. On Saturday evening, November 10, 1984, the Taylors entertained Teresa's cousin, her husband, and their baby in their Manalapan, New Jersey, home. The visiting couple noticed that Ken seemed nervous and anxious for them to leave, even helping the couple gather their child's things. He insisted on carrying the playpen from the den to the car, and they saw this as unusual for Ken. That night, in their 23 Valley Road home, Ken killed Teresa. When the awful truth about Teresa's disappearance became undeniable, Teresa's mother's first words were, "He did it to her again."

Teresa did not appear the next day for the Sunday christening of her friend's baby. Ken called and said, without apparent emotion, that Teresa was spaced out on codeine and cocaine and had finally faced up to her addiction. That morning he had dropped her off at the Newark Airport. He explained that she would be gone for three or four weeks. When she was settled, she would call. He couldn't say where she was. Teresa was strong-willed and had wanted it this way.

Ken explained that he was en route to Indiana with the baby because Teresa did not want to burden her mother with his care. Ken wanted Teresa's parents to be told that the family was on a short vacation to Indiana so they would not worry. "Cancel my appointments," and Ken was off the line.

Worry? Everyone was frantic with worry, except perhaps the local police department where the initial response was that wives' disappearances are usually short-lived. "The wife just wants to leave her family for awhile." In this case, no domestic violence was involved, and the police counseled patience.

When Teresa's father telephoned Ken's parents in Indiana, he learned that they were expecting Ken. Ken had called from Columbus, Ohio, to say he had been delayed but was on his way. His parents told the same story about Teresa having left for drug addiction treatment.

While still en route to Indiana Ken called the Benignos, telling them he probably should have gone with Teresa instead of leaving her at the airport, but there was nothing to do now. The baby was fine. Anyway, Teresa had promised to call in a couple of days and then everything would be straightened out. Teresa's father later said that talking to Ken was like "punching air." He begged his son-in-law to call the police. Ken agreed that he would do it as soon as he returned from his trip.

Teresa's father then called the police, and he and Teresa's sister traveled to the Valley Road home. What struck them immediately was that the remains of the cake Teresa had served on Saturday evening were still on the kitchen counter, uncovered. Teresa always kept things neat and would never have left food out in this way. Her keys were on the coffee table. Teresa's sister fed the kittens who were mewing with hunger.

Ken was slow to return from Indiana, telephoning that he had taken a wrong turn and been caught in traffic. He asked if anyone had heard from Teresa. The Benignos told him they had learned that

Teresa might have gone to Michigan to visit a friend, and Ken seized on that. He said he was too tired to report her missing that night, but promised to go to the police the following morning (Thursday). He slept in the Valley Road home.

The next day, at the Benigno home on Staten Island, Ken started to cry in their shared misery. He said he hadn't eaten all day, and Teresa's mother fixed him a sandwich. (Later he would say that she forced food on him.) Ken complained that he didn't understand how his wife "could do this to us."

When Ken learned that the family had been to his home, he was indignant, asking, "How come you guys were at my place?" When he was told that they were looking for something to explain Teresa's disappearance, they noted a condescending smirk on Ken's face. He had no way of knowing that a forensic test would show blood, incredible amounts of blood, on the first floor of the New Jersey house. No mop and pail clean-up could remove the evidence.

When the police were informed about the Acapulco incident, one member of the department in particular became suspicious of Ken. The husband seemed too smooth. The wife had not taken her toothbrush, and the officer had always found this to be an ominous sign. Her closet was neat and orderly. When asked about her possible reasons for leaving, Ken said his wife had been depressed about the pressures of new motherhood. There was no mention of Teresa going to the "hospital" for "drug treatment."

After murdering Teresa, Ken took a four-day odyssey. All the while, unbelievably, Teresa's body lay in the trunk of his car. Ken stayed in touch with both families, keeping contact but sharing nothing real with anybody. What was he doing during those four days?

First, after the killing, he stuffed the body in the trunk, then he cleaned up the blood. After the televised Jets game finished, he called his parents to say he was coming. With the baby beside him, and Teresa's body in the trunk, he left Manalapan for his parents' home, making a couple of stops along the way. In Indiana his father offered to help unload the car's trunk, but Ken said there was no need and he held onto the key.

He gave the baby to his mother, and he talked about Teresa. His parents could not imagine what it must have been like to live with a wife on drugs. Later Ken's father attributed his daughter-in-law's death to a drug overdose. Although Ken said he would stay with his parents for two or three days, he took off the next morning. After he had left, in her top vanity drawer, his mother found a $20 bill with a note saying, "Love, Ken."

At Marilyn's house, with Teresa's body still in the car trunk, he informed Marilyn that it was "definitely finished" between him and Teresa. He announced, "things just didn't work out." Later, in Pennsylvania, on his way home to New Jersey he disposed of Teresa's body. When her body was discovered, Marilyn traveled to New York to be with Ken, but she soon left. Belatedly, she severed her connection to Ken.

The night he returned to New Jersey, the same evening he had said he was too tired to contact the police about his wife's whereabouts, Ken's fatigue was not so great that he could not make other calls. His telephone record showed calls to a massage parlor. What he actually did that night was to head for a Staten Island go-go club featuring naked dancers.

Later, after confessing to the murder, he described himself as trying to commit suicide on that evening, but he said the hose fell off the car exhaust and he had second thoughts about suicide. It would be irresponsible to leave his children fatherless.

At the police station, Ken appeared nonchalant at first. He was willing to waive his rights, and he showed no sign of unease. He appeared anxious to be of assistance and properly cooperative. He mentioned nothing about Acapulco or his previous marriages. He described his marriage as happy, but he said his wife had a growing drug addiction problem. After the Acapulco story came out, he talked of Teresa's depression after childbirth without commenting on the drug problem he had first mentioned. Even when police found a bloody earring on his garage floor Ken did not crack. A stranger could have done it, he said.

Finally, Ken asked the officer what he would do if he found his wife giving his infant son fellatio. When asked if that was what had happened, Ken said, yes, and began to cry. This was to be Ken's defense. Unable to sleep, he came downstairs early in the morning to find his son on the dining room table with his wife bent over the baby.

Ken went on to say that he was fed up with Teresa's drug use, and when he found her sexually abusing their son, this was the last straw. He yelled at his wife and chased her to the laundry room. He claimed that she grabbed his dumbbell bar and swung it at him. He ducked and, to defend himself, he wrested the bar away from her. Then, he sobbed, "I gave it to her." When asked if he hit his wife more than once, he asked irritably, "What kind of question is that?" Of course he swung more than once. At this point Ken finally asked for a lawyer.

Teresa's body was found in Pennsylvania about 50 miles from the New Jersey border at the base of Hart Mountain. The body was found in a bird sanctuary, wrapped in gray carpet padding, the same padding Teresa's cousin remembered seeing in the first floor guest room of the Taylor home. That evening it was rolled up because the room was being renovated. The wrapped body had been stuffed inside a tan sleeping bag. Massive head injuries had been inflicted with a blunt instrument. Nine shattering blows to her face and head had broken the back of her skull into three pieces. Her brain tissue oozed out between the skull fragments.

The white sweater and beige culottes were the same ones Teresa was wearing that Saturday evening when she entertained her cousin. There was the gold watch, the wedding band, and one diamond earring. One upper front tooth (capped after the Acapulco incident) had been knocked out from the blows. The other had a fragment of the original tooth remaining as if the cap (also resulting from the Acapulco attack) had been knocked off. Her culottes were torn in back and had been pulled down below her hips. Her anus and vagina were found to have been smeared with vaseline.

In prison, unable to raise $500,000 bail, Ken explained his delay in disposing of the body. His mother wondered why he was not afraid of an accident or the police. His response was that he was driving carefully because he had his son with him. He delayed dumping the body because he loved his wife and didn't want to part with her. He kept her as long as he could. He didn't know what to do. Teresa liked the outdoors. She liked birds.

Ken was suddenly angry that his parents had brought the baby to see him. Didn't they understand why he had brought the baby to Indiana? Later his parents would say, "Kenny wants us to have him. There is nothing to discuss." Ken was determined not to let Teresa's "dingbat" sister have the baby. Many months, thousands of dollars, and dozens of trips to Indiana were required before Teresa's sister and her husband obtained custody of Teresa's baby who had been taken from New Jersey illegally. The baby was finally returned to New York to share the home of his aunt and uncle and two small cousins.

From prison, Ken tirelessly wrote letters to his parents and to Marilyn, professing love, threatening suicide, and assuring Marilyn that she should not feel guilty if her relationship with Ken had pushed Teresa into drugs.

A defense psychiatrist testified that Ken was planning to kill his wife because she wouldn't respond to him sexually. He was getting more response from ads in magazines than from his wife. Also, his wife was a constant nag. More likely Ken's fierce need to control his wife, financial chaos, and his underlying generalized restless rage played more of a role. It is possible that Teresa was beginning to "catch on" and raise questions. In any case, Ken was finished with Teresa and the life she had created for them. And there was the $100,000 insurance for the baby.

The Benignos were dumbfounded to discover that their daughter's murder took place inside the house, that her body was dragged from the laundry room down the hall, across the living room, and by the very sofa and chairs on which they sat to discuss their daughter's disappearance. The bloody trail was 55 feet long.

Richard Crafts

The heartlessly planned "woodchipper murder" was cleverly executed and was solved only because of a private investigator's extraordinary persistence. Despite suspicions, the Eastern Airline pilot's murder of his flight attendant wife could easily have gone undetected.

Why did he want to kill the blonde woman who seemed the ideal wife and loving mother? The fundamental reason was that he simply did not need her anymore. Even worse, she was in his way. And she was asking uncomfortable questions, even considering divorcing him. Divorce was a problem for Richard, an expensive one.

Better that he should live with his three children and the vehicle-strewn yard and have his freedom without complaints from his wife. If only she would just disappear . . . there might even be airline insurance. . . . He viewed the messy divorce route as inconvenient as well as expensive. He had said as much to his brother-in-law, asking advice on how to "squirrel away" assets.

And so, exhibiting no apparent response or the usual qualms of conscience for his children's pain, this man took control of his wife's destiny. Later, when confronted, he blamed the dead woman, attempting to destroy her reputation. This, after chipping her body to bits.

Richard Crafts's murder plans required several steps, each of which he meticulously followed. At his home on 5 Newfield Lane in Newtown, Connecticut, he had plenty of space on his 2.6-acre house lot for his new car, the new dump truck he had ordered, two riding lawn mowers, a backhoe, a snow blower, a cement mixer, a tractor, and welding equipment. There was also room for the rented U-Haul truck and woodchipper.

The home in the upper-middle-class neighborhood was in disrepair, both inside and out, and crammed with Richard's equipment. He had a large gun collection, and during the months before his wife's murder he spent $5,000 on guns alone. He considered all property his to do with as he wished, regardless of his wife's concerns.

The Crafts couple owned an additional 2.6-acre lot on the next street, giving Richard still more flexibility in his murder plans. There was the new freezer big enough for his wife's body, and an electric generator to keep it frozen solid for chipping. His wife's murder may have been one of the few unqualified successes of Richard's life. Yet, while he had left no obvious clues, his behavior after the murder—as well as before—raised suspicions in all who knew the couple, including his sister.

Possibly he neither knew nor cared because he thought he had committed the "perfect crime." His wife Helle had gone on a "trip." It was true that he had not expected a blow on the head with a flashlight to produce so much blood, thereby requiring him to dispose of all that blood-soaked bedding and carpet. But who would expect anyone to search the landfill or be able to find anything there if they did?

The purchased dump truck arrived late, but he was able to rent a U-Haul truck to use instead. The truck was seen parked on the bridge with a woodchipper, but he could find a reason, even if it was 4 a.m. on a snowy November morning. That 4 a.m. sighting was a factor in Richard's trial, but, in general, the snow had been a help because fewer people were on the road.

Richard's children were visiting his brother-in-law's family in a nearby town for a couple of days after Helle's disappearance, giving him plenty of time to tow Helle's car to the Pan Am parking lot. Her car in the lot helped support his story that his wife had gone on a "trip." His scheme had succeeded.

The sequence of events had begun to unfold on the evening of November 18, 1986. After her return from an international flight, her fellow flight attendants dropped her off at her wooded Connecticut home on the dead-end circle. The time was about 7 p.m., the last time she was seen alive.

Reconstructing the scene from the evidence, we know Helle put on a blue nightgown. She was bending over the mattress to make the bed when Richard apparently came from behind. He hit her over the head with a flashlight, a weapon that would not have alarmed her had she turned around. The three children were asleep in their beds, and the live-in babysitter was away from the house at her evening job.

Richard placed Helle's body in the freezer and moved the freezer to the nearby lot he had purchased. The generator provided the electricity to freeze her body. Late the next night he used a chain saw to chop her body into several pieces which he placed in trash bags. The darkness and snow of the isolated area helped him work unobserved. He even appeared at the police station for duty as a town auxiliary police officer.

Finally, a woodchipper disposed of bone, flesh, teeth and the blonde hair of his wife. He put the body through the chipper with a load of wood, apparently to clean the chipper and disperse the evidence. Later, along the roadside and in the river near the bridge were found blue fibers from her nightgown along with bits of bone, teeth, and even a piece of her toe.

The husband disposed of the bloody mattress, bedding, and carpet in the town landfill and bought new bedding and carpet, including new carpeting for the children's rooms. Pieces of the bloody carpet were found in the town landfill only because a search was instigated at the insistence of Helle's fellow flight attendants and the private investigator involved in the pending divorce. All refused to accept the husband's explanation that Helle was either a "missing person" or had gone to visit her "sick mother."

Richard's behavior after the murder raised suspicion. Helle's friends had last seen her on Tuesday. When her fellow flight attendant called Helle on Wednesday, Richard said she was not home. Thursday she was still not home and his story was that Helle had phoned from London and said that her mother was ill. Richard gave a wrong number for Helle's mother in Denmark. When the mother was finally reached she said she was not ill and not expecting a visit from her daughter.

On Saturday, Helle's car was still in the Pan Am parking lot, and her flight attendant friends feared for her job. A week went by and Richard still did not call the airline to request a leave of absence for his wife. Nine days passed. She did not return for Thanksgiving. Helle, who always called her children when she was away, had not returned or called for the holiday. Her friends were frantic but Richard appeared unconcerned. Now he said that she might be at Club Med in the Canary Islands or in Florida. He thought she might be annoyed if he reported her as a "missing person." Also, he said he was busy with the children's teacher conferences.

By December 3rd he said his wife had run off with her "Oriental boyfriend" and he did not want to air the family's dirty linen in public. The stories he concocted were not even remotely plausible, but he appeared unaware that he was arousing suspicion rather than diverting it. All felt certain that Richard knew where Helle was. Still, whatever he had done, it appeared he would get away with it.

Other actions did not "add up." Surprisingly, Richard allowed a paper trail of his large purchases and his telephone calls to a woman friend to accumulate even as the marriage moved toward divorce. Was the evidence of his purchases and his talks with the "other woman" in New Jersey part of his arrogant disregard for his wife, a way to harass and abuse her? It could also be a way to control her, to bring her to a more submissive posture in her futile attempts to make this puzzling marriage work.

Richard's spending is known to have worried his wife. Helle paid most household and childcare expenses from her salary, even though Richard earned three times as much as she did. Despite Richard's substantial salary as an airline pilot and their dual income, the Crafts had no more than a few thousand dollars in the bank. Helle earned extra money selling Shaklee products and running a small lace curtain business from her home. Her friends said Helle sewed many of her children's clothes. She could hardly have been happy when, shortly before her death, she noted that Richard had purchased a new car.

After the murder, the paper trail continued. Records of his purchases and rentals were easily available, including new bedding and carpeting to replace the bloody evidence he had taken to the landfill. The children's nanny confirmed that the master bedroom carpeting, which had been replaced after Helle's disappearance, was still new.

The story of Richard and Helle's lives was investigated by Herzog (1989). From his description of their courtship and marriage it is clear that there were serious danger signals. Helle had long been vulnerable to financial abuse, emotional abuse, and physical injury, whether or not death resulted. Although Richard was known for his characteristic secretiveness, probably even he did not know, with certainty, the outcome of the marriage until a few weeks before his wife's death.

Getting rid of his wife was Richard's response to Helle's reluctant but increasing seriousness in her desire for a divorce, a step that would disturb the convenience of his life. When Helle contacted a lawyer, Richard's words to his wife were a non-committal "anything you want," but he refused to allow himself to be served with legal papers. A divorce would increase Helle's independence and give her new controls over him, his finances, and his access to the children. He might have to pay child support and the court might even require him to pay the mortgage on a house he could no longer live in. This was in September, two months before the murder.

Despite her lawyer's warning, Helle informed Richard that she had obtained pictures of him (taken by a hired private investigator) as he left his woman friend's house. Helle had mistakenly hoped that the information would encourage Richard to mend his ways. Instead, he was enraged, and even more so when he learned that she had gone through his papers to discover the new car he had bought.

Richard's sister publicly stated her opinion that his wife's invasion of his privacy was the final straw. His sister also said that she first suspected her brother's involvement as soon as she heard his story about Helle having abandoned their children. She knew Helle so well that this lie was obvious. Her testimony against her brother helped convict him.

Jack Levin, Professor of Sociology at Northeastern University, states that the major difficulty with avoiding sociopaths is in detecting them (*Boston Herald*, Jan. 14, 1990). They are experts at deluding others. If they show any obvious sign it may be their possessiveness and egocentricity. Also, their lies are often too good to be true. Hindsight often allows a clearer view into the hoaxes they perpetrate.

An additional difficulty is that wives are acculturated to pleasing their husbands at all costs. Because they have not learned to recognize abuse, they often see their pain and marriage problems as resulting from their own failures as women and wives.

Helle occasionally mentioned marital problems to her fellow flight attendants, usually in a superficial way without serious complaints. They knew things were not going well, that she was considering divorce. It is doubtful that anyone used the harsh and scary word "abuse." Helle's friends later described her as naive, although to at least five people she said, "If anything happens to me, don't think it was an accident."

Helle had no control over the household. She tried to persuade her husband to repair the house, attend some of the children's school functions, and stop seeing his woman friend. When he demanded that she pay for her car with cash instead of using the airline credit union she complied. His control was so complete that he would not let her leave the marriage alive.

More than once her friends observed her blackened eyes, but Helle made light of their observation. In 1977, in the presence of friends, Helle mildly challenged something her husband said. Without warning, Richard struck her, knocking her to the floor. He remained impassive and no one ever spoke of the incident. Her friends later said that Richard made them uneasy. He seemed in a "dream world." They observed that Helle seemed to need to boost Richard's ego as well as her own.

During their courtship her husband alternately rejected and charmed her. Sometimes he left her for months. He was always with women, but he was non-selective, using them for his satisfaction only. Women were attracted to him and sought him out. He saw a wife, it is said, as primarily a breeder. When Helle became pregnant, he pushed her to get an abortion. Then he changed his mind and decided to marry her. He voiced doubts about whether the baby was really his. Helle was kept continually confused and off-balance.

After the marriage, Richard used his home in Connecticut as a cheap and convenient base of operations. He also kept the New York apartment he had before the marriage, including the furniture, and he continued seeing other women. Although Richard was tight with money for his family, he lavished money on other women and on the assorted vehicles he owned. His hair was unkempt and he wore the clothes of a woodsman. He consumed one or two six-packs of beer a day.

Neighbors saw Richard as a man who kept to himself, spending much of his time working outside on projects he never finished. He was willing to be helpful to neighbors but made no friends. Neighbors saw Helle as a patient mother who made her children's Halloween costumes and taught them to swim and ski. When Richard did not show up for the birth of one of her children, she drove herself to the hospital rather than ask a neighbor to drive her. In spite of her three children, Helle appeared psychologically alone and adrift.

The summer before the murder occurred, Richard had colon cancer surgery. He lied to his wife about the prognosis, instead he claimed that his case was serious and that he did not have long to live. Helle set aside thoughts of divorce to take care of him, especially when he promised to be a better husband and father. To her friends the usually outgoing and upbeat Helle seemed isolated, edgy, and remote.

When Richard was arrested on January 13th, 1987, he asked his lawyer to find evidence of major flaws in Helle's character. Untruthfully, he claimed that Helle's parents were not married until she was 25. Not that it should have had any bearing on the case, even if true, but he sought ways to discredit the dead woman as if this might somehow excuse his crime.

In a vain attempt to divert attention to another perpetrator he claimed that the chain saw used on Helle's body was stolen from his unlocked house. The evidence made this defense futile. Richard Crafts was sentenced to 50 years in prison. He is appealing his case.

He sought custody of the children, wanting them sent to Florida to his mother. Instead, custody was awarded to Richard's sister and her husband in Connecticut. Only his mother in Florida continues to support Richard's innocence. For others it was only too clear "who done it." It was the husband.

Jeffrey MacDonald

Court psychiatrists described Jeffrey MacDonald as a sociopath. He is a convicted wife murderer whose case was widely publicized. Court testimony, tapes, including those of McGinniss, (1983), provide insight into his mind and the circumstances of this case.

After Jeff's conviction and incarceration, McGinniss spent several months interviewing him in prison, recording their conversations, going through Jeff's voluminous papers, and interviewing those who knew him. While Jeff was in prison, McGinniss lived in Jeff's California condo for a time.

In 1991, ten years after conviction, MacDonald continued his tireless fight to overturn his sentence and exonerate himself, contending that evidence of hair and clothing of non-family members found in the apartment was suppressed at his trial. Many people continue to be persuaded that he is innocent and should be released, and he was even promised his old job as physician in a West Coast hospital. His appeal, however, was denied.

Although his wife Colette's expectations that her own needs be fulfilled were, from all accounts, not high, the marriage could not have been easy. She denied, or learned to overlook, the controlling behaviors she experienced from Jeff. She may even have misread them as signs of Jeff's husbandly concern for his family. Like the cases previously described, her goal was a successful marriage. And, as in the Crafts case, hindsight makes the dangerous pattern of his behavior clearer.

Colette is described as the kind of person who would always make everything seem right. She would never expose a problem or unhappiness that would reflect poorly on Jeff or their marriage. She would feel hurt, but she would not fight or argue.

It is conjectured that the precipitating event for her murder may have been what might, on the surface, seem minor. Dr. Jeffrey MacDonald may have felt his authority challenged by his wife's proffered information. Although she was known as an accommo- dating wife, she may have tried out some of the material she had learned in the psychology class she attended the evening of her murder. Her class notes of that evening tend to corroborate this opinion. The two had disagreed on how to handle the bed-wetting problem of their five-year-old daughter, Kimberly.

Evidence used to reconstruct the crime makes it appear likely that the fight started in the bedroom when he struck her with a piece of shelving from their daughter's room. As in most spouse murders, there is no eyewitness, but evidence shows that both Colette's arms were broken during her attempt to ward off the attack. And then there were the knives, the ice pick, and the ensuing massacre of the whole family—Colette, Kimberly and Kristen. Colette was found beside the bed, lying on her back, with her chest covered by Jeff's pajama top except for an exposed breast. One of her eyes was open.

The motive appears unrelated to money or to a rival for Colette's affections, but rather to extreme, violent rage. Jeffrey, the family man living in a cramped military apartment and stationed at Fort Bragg, North Carolina, had apparently destroyed his entire family during that rainy night.

Jeff presents himself as an egocentric and extremely possessive, but not violent, man. It would appear impossible, without under- standing his character, that he could stab his pregnant wife in the chest 26 times with an ice pick and seven times with a knife, stab her nine times in the neck, and break both her arms.

Jeff sought escape from the consequences of the crime with his claim that the murders resulted from drug-crazed intruders, the story which he continues to tell today. There were inconsistencies in his accounts and in his arrangement of the crime scene. Nevertheless, despite suspicions, he remained a free man for several years.

During the months preceding her February murder, Colette's parents noted that she seemed depressed. She made no complaints about her husband, but that would have been uncharacteristic. At the time, without other explanation, her parents attributed her fatigue and lack of energy to a difficult third pregnancy. When they invited Colette to spend Christmas with them, her response was a tired, "Wait until spring."

The preceding Christmas, without telling his wife, Jeff bought a surprise pony for the children. Only two months later, five-year-old Kimberly's skull was shattered with two blows to the right side of her head. When the blood was later washed off, the hole was described as the size of the "Grand Canyon." Kim was clubbed on the left side of her head, leaving her cheek bone protruding through the skin. She was stabbed in the neck with a knife eight to ten times, and the knife was passed through her windpipe. Two-and-a-half-year-old Kristen received 33 wounds. She was stabbed 12 times in the back with a knife and four times in the chest as well as the neck. The ice pick inflicted 15 puncture wounds in Kristen's chest.

The bloody rampage went far beyond the violence needed to kill the three victims (and the four-month-old fetus). The very rage might, for some, have substantiated Jeff's story of drug-crazed intruders as the killers. The killer could not be the husband of his high school sweetheart and the father who had recently bought a surprise pony for his daughter. His medical associates expressed the opinion that Jeff could not have done it, that he was not capable of it. One said, "He was the best student I ever had."

Jeff's explanation of events appeared plausible and it was not impossible that what he described did occur. He had the further advantage of being a dedicated and respected military officer. In the military trial that followed the slayings, he was cleared. However, his wound was so minor and was almost professionally performed; it might have been self-inflicted to divert suspicion. Surgery was a special interest of Jeff's and he hoped for more training in this area. While the wound penetrated the lung, it was in a place where it would do the least damage. Another puzzling fact was that a different knife, a dull Geneva Forge knife, caused his wound, while the one used on his family was described as a sharp Old Hickory knife.

The very violence of the attacks on the woman and children turned attention toward Jeff. The opinion was expressed that he might have exploded after "domestic stress," but that he posed no threat to others.

Each of the four family members had a different blood type, making it easier to reconstruct the last moments of the murdered members of the MacDonald family. The bloody trail portrayed an eerie picture, including Colette's rush to the bedroom of two-year-old Kristen in a vain attempt to protect her.

It is true that important evidence in the MacDonald case was lost. For example, Jeff's blue pajama bottoms were discarded in the hospital. The garbage was collected and the sewage was not checked. The result was a possible loss of evidence, including the surgical gloves that were used to write the word "pig" with blood on the bedroom wall. The skin taken from beneath Colette's fingernails was inexplicably lost as well as the vial containing blue fibers from beneath Kristen's fingernails. After the crime, the living room furniture was straightened, and this was the room by the apartment door where Jeff claimed he was attacked. If there was ever any evidence of disarray here, it was lost.

Blood was present in all three bedrooms, but none was observed in the living room where Jeff was supposedly attacked. How did Kim's blood get on his pajama top when he said he had removed it and placed it over Colette's body before going to Kim's room? Why did the ice pick wounds on Colette's chest match ice pick holes in the pajama top, indicating that he used the ice pick after he put his pajama top over Colette? Was the pajama top put over Colette to explain the fact that the blood on it was not Jeff's but Colette's?

Jeff's story was that his pajama top was torn in the living room struggle with the intruders. However, when the pieces of the pajama top were later realigned, there was a contiguous pattern of stain. This indicated that the stain was there during the struggle with Colette before it was torn. Knowing that it was her blood type on his pajama top, he placed it over her dead body to explain the presence of his wife's blood on his pajama top.

Jeff said he was at the kitchen sink, but no blood was found in the kitchen. He claimed that he stopped giving his daughter, Kim, mouth-to-mouth resuscitation because he saw that air was bubbling out of her chest. Kim had no chest wounds.

Evidence showed that Jeff's wound occurred at the bathroom sink. Standing in front of the bathroom mirror, the apparently self-inflicted wound was expertly done so that damage was minimal and recovery quick.

If drug-crazed intruders struck him from above, according to his story, why were there no observable injuries to his head and shoulders? He claimed he was sleeping in the living room because Kim had wet the double bed where he slept with Colette, but the pillow he always used was not in the living room. And, when Kim wet the bed, it was known that it was Colette who customarily moved to the living room. If, as he said, the major struggle with the "druggies" had occurred in the living room, why could no blood or other corroborating sign be found?

Jeff denied the presence of an ice pick in the home, but Colette's mother remembered seeing it at Christmas when she and her husband visited the MacDonald family. In fact, her mother remembered using it.

Jeff's reason for not calling the neighbors after the attack was that he "didn't know them that well." Jeff's first call for assistance was recorded at the military base at 3:40 a.m. At 3:42 a.m. he made a second call that was also recorded. Jeff's description of his activities during that two-minute time interval included going outside to look for the intruders, going into the bathroom to check his wounds and wash his hands, looking into the hall closet for medical supplies, returning to the master bedroom to check his wife for signs of life, administering mouth-to-mouth resuscitation, and checking for pulses at various points on each of the three bodies. How could he have done so much in two minutes?

The MacDonald family history describes Jeff's father as an angry man who constantly railed against domination by women and talked about women wanting to rule and "take over." When he drove his car, other drivers on the road frequently infuriated him. From his two sons he demanded obedience and achievement, and anything else he declared to be weakness. The father is portrayed as one who was subject to sudden outbursts of anger and one who did not show affection to anyone.

Jeff's mother continued to believe in her son's innocence. After his conviction she spent long periods of time in California to be with him. Jeff gave his mother clippings about the case and the trial which she carefully pasted in her scrapbook. Jeff was especially proud when his case made the front page of *The New York Times*.

In high school Jeff was voted the most popular and likely to succeed. He courted Colette during her college years, writing longing letters to which she responded in kind. She left college before graduating in order to marry Jeff. Colette followed him from one cramped apartment to another while he went through an Ivy League college and on to medical school. Following graduation from medical school he volunteered to serve as a Green Beret in the U.S. Marines. To outside observers it would seem that Jeff had achieved the success he sought. How could he have done so well for so long?

This was the "public" Jeff. At home he was known to be highly critical of his wife, and while she was a teenager he had once been observed to strike Colette. During the marriage, and before, there were always other women. There was one woman in particular whom he visited on the day before his wedding to Colette as well as the day after the birth of his first child.

While she was pregnant with their first child, Colette expressed interest in having natural childbirth but Jeff took charge and advised her against it. He told her he knew she couldn't do it. When she went into labor he did not remain with her, saying he saw no reason to stay. Colette was anesthetized and the result was a cesarean birth. When she awakened and asked him about the baby, he told her that the baby did not look all that pretty.

When Colette's mother came to help her daughter after the birth, Jeff was mildly critical of his mother-in-law's housekeeping, telling an associate that he was the one "clearly in charge of the family."

After the murder, with much emotion and tears about his lost family, Jeff said to his wife's parents, "They are all I had . . . I couldn't protect her. She was so good and you gave her to me and I couldn't take care of her." Colette's parents received a shipment of clothing that had belonged to Colette and their granddaughters. It was from Jeff. During the following months there was no further word from him except a cheery "wish you were here" travel post-card.

Colette's parents were left alone with their grief, they sat silently in their home and told friends sadly that "nothing would ever be worth saying again." Colette had been their only child, arriving after three stillbirths, and each of the dead babies had also been named "Colette." Now, at 26, the fourth Colette was dead.

Almost a year passed before Colette's father began to suspect the unthinkable: his daughter's and granddaughters' murderer was his son-in-law. Originally a staunch supporter of Jeff, his doubts mounted to near certainty. He sought answers to questions. When answers were unsatisfactory or unavailable, he instigated a pains-taking investigation. Jeff's story was good, almost too good, but it did not "add up." Jeff's behavior after the murder did not "add up" either. The struggle to put Jeffrey MacDonald behind bars took ten long years.

The military Criminal Investigation Unit had cleared MacDonald soon after the killings, but enormous perseverance was required to obtain the transcripts. Sensing his father-in-law's frustration with the delay, Jeff announced that on November 16th, nine months after the murder, he had personally participated in the killing of one of the "hippies" who had attacked him and his family. No po-lice report supports this. Possibly Jeff hoped that avenging the crime would derail the single-minded purpose of his in-laws. It did the opposite.

Jeff's account of his life at 544 Castle Drive in Fayetteville, North Carolina, before the murders revealed conflicting informa-tion. What he said was that life was finally more settled, giving him time to "re-attach" to his family. His hours were now shorter and he was no longer tired. There was a discrepancy between his per-ception and what was later discovered about his activities.

It was later found that, before the February murders, Jeff worked every January night moonlighting at Cape Fear Valley Hospital in Fayetteville. He was also doing weekend shifts at Hamlet Hospital, 60 miles away. In fact, he was seeking still a third moonlighting job. On February 16th, the very day of the murder, he called a pediatrician to discuss moonlighting in Lumberton, North Carolina!

It was speculated that Jeff may have used amphetamines to maintain his high energy level and to help control weight gain. In 1970 there was little indication that this was harmful, and no tests for amphetamines were done while he was in the hospital recovering from his wound.

Jeff, well muscled and just under six feet tall, enjoyed boxing workouts on the military base. He was so good at them that he was invited to become team physician. He told Colette that he would be away for a while that spring because he was going to Russia with the boxing team. It was later found that there were no plans for the team to travel to Russia.

After the murders and before he was cleared by the military investigation, he lived on base at the Bachelor Officer Quarters. While at the "BOQ" he entered into a sexual relationship with a woman he met there. There would be other women as well. In California he began a relationship with a friend of his mother's. On two occasions the woman's ten-year-old son encountered Jeff's terrifying rage, and once on a boating excursion he feared for his life. Jeff had threatened to drown him. The woman immediately ended her relationship with Jeff.

Four years were required to obtain an indictment, and for four more years the MacDonald attorneys fought to have it dismissed. He took his legal battles to the U.S. Supreme Court which ruled that he had not been denied his constitutional right to a speedy trial. He was unsuccessful in his attempt to obtain a presidential pardon.

In the meantime, Jeff acquired a California oceanfront condo, an expensive foreign car, a 34-foot yacht, and many new friends. In California he worked in a hospital emergency room where he had a special interest in treating abused children. He was an instructor in the UCLA Medical School and author of a text on emergency medical technology. He was president of the South Carolina Heart Association.

Before he was tried in North Carolina, a California pre-trial party was held for Jeff. The Long Beach Police Officers Association was involved, and everyone spoke admiringly of Jeff—friends, girlfriends, his college roommate. There was disco music and a gourmet feast. Admission was $100, and $500 entitled admission to the Golden Circle. The money was used to support Jeff's defense. His friends willingly took over the payments on his boat, condo, and car. They shared his view that the incarceration was no more than a temporary setback. Soon he would return and the party would continue.

With Jeff finally in prison in 1980, the case was still not over. Jeff continued to write explanatory letters to everyone. He wrote daily letters to his biographer McGinniss. He initiated contacts for publicity about his case.

On Jeff's 36th birthday, friends and former colleagues rented an airplane to fly over the prison trailing a banner saying, "Happy Birthday, Rock." This was the nickname he had acquired in the hospital emergency room as a tribute to his coolness and steadiness under pressure.

The exhaustive psychiatric evaluation done in connection with this case identified risk factors in Jeff's personality. Jeff is an articulate man, and from the beginning he was willing and eager to talk at length to establish his credibility. The reports described him as charming and engaging on the surface, a man who exhibited extreme egocentricity and possessiveness with an absence of interest and empathy for others. He appeared to see himself as having the right to control and possess others, and he was able to exploit them without guilt. He demonstrated haughty, grandiose, and controlling responses. His narcissism was described as typically well controlled but potentially openly raging.

Information about Jeff describes his inability to acknowledge or experience guilt or mourning. It was said that he attempted to compensate himself for the rage and envy he experienced with fantasies of wealth, beauty, and omnipotence. Accompanying the boundless, repressed rage was the image presented of self-deprecating humor and calculating seductiveness combined with pseudo self-insight. Avoidance of close involvement with others prevented release of the existing intense rage.

The team's damning report cast doubt on Jeff's credibility and discussed the facade he presented that concealed the absence of deep emotional response. He was described as bereft of conscience, incapable of emotional closeness or a mutually cooperative relationship with a woman, and out of touch with his feelings. The report continued with reference to his inability to profit from experience, disdain for those with whom he differed, inability to face reality, and denial of the truth. Also noted was his need for attention and approval.

The bottom line, repeated in various ways, was that Jeff was a character-disordered individual, a sociopath subject to violence under pressure.

Steven Steinberg

Frondorf's investigation (1988) of Steven Steinberg's life, both before and after his wife's murder, makes clear the destructive patterns in his apparently successful life.

After knowing Steve for years, Elana was only beginning to suspect her husband's problems. Speculation about the reason for her murder at this point in the marriage focuses on a likely precipitating factor: Elana was beginning to uncover her husband's lies about their uncertain financial condition.

Despite the viciousness of the murder, Steve was not known to be a violent man. In hindsight, however, there were risk factors that might have indicated what lay ahead. Although he was not convicted, there was never any question about "who done it."

While employed as a manager at his father-in-law's restaurant, Steve was known for an occasional flare-up of anger with suppliers. He was a master at avoiding paying suppliers' overdue bills and frequently attempted to intimidate them with his "lawyers." Employees in the restaurant often felt pushed around by Steve's barked peremptory orders. Once he threatened an employee with a knife, a fact that never emerged during his trial. However, to the customers, many of whom were Scottsdale's finest, he was all charm — attentive to their needs, finding the best table for each, greeting old customers by name, and telling them exactly what he knew they wanted to hear.

Near the end of Elana's life, the Steinbergs stopped at Lake Tahoe during a vacation trip. It was in May, just 13 days before Elana was killed. When Elana attempted to block Steve from taking all of their money to the gambling casino, he shoved her against the motel door. This is the only documented incident of physical violence he inflicted on his wife — except for the murder. Elana telephoned her mother, frantic to be left in the motel room with no cash. The next day Steve returned with money from somewhere, and their trip continued. In court his obsessive gambling was presented as little more than a harmless pastime and escape from his nagging wife.

In addition to the gambling obsession, his affable exterior concealed a demanding, controlling personality, but it is doubtful that Elana knew how precarious her existence actually was. Her life had been at risk for years and she hadn't known it.

Steve made friends easily, exhibiting an easygoing humor and charm. Some said he looked like a young Tony Curtis. He lived well, entering enthusiastically into the upscale life of their social circle in sunny, suburban Scottsdale. The new environment was a welcome change from the constricted life in a middle-class section of Chicago where he and Elana grew up. In Chicago, and later in Arizona, the couple remained close to Elana's mother, father, and brother whose move to Arizona had preceded theirs. It was a life that suited Steve perfectly. But Steve always needed more money. There was never enough.

Although he was a clever and glib salesman, the jobs he obtained on his own had never lasted for long because his shortcuts and manipulation of the truth made his employers uncomfortable. All agreed, however, that he was a feverishly hard worker with boundless energy who was willing to put in long hours.

Beginning in his night school years, when he also began gambling, he was a restless workaholic. Frondorf (1988) comments on the seam of anger and impulse in Steve. During the marriage, his father-in-law supplied his employment, and, until their first daughter was born, Elana worked as a legal secretary.

Steve and Elana appeared as the perfect couple, good-looking, hard-working, and successful. Their two daughters were smart and pretty, and Elana was a devoted mother. The Steinbergs had many friends and enjoyed an active social life in affluent Scottsdale. Elana's whole existence was centered on the family's well-being. She was a talented hostess and loving mother who accommodated her own life to the needs of her husband and two daughters.

Her friends noted that she built her husband's self-esteem and made him feel good, and that she would tolerate no criticism of her husband. If her brother and her husband disagreed about a business matter, Elana always supported her husband. That was what a wife did. Perhaps she also expected that her devotion would help appease her husband's underlying restlessness. Elana's personality was spirited, lively, outgoing, and forthright. The support she gave her husband was neither fearful nor submissive. She was an intelligent woman.

Although she was smart, she wanted very much to believe her husband's stories. He always had an explanation. Only when the problem was his infidelity did she stand up to him, making it clear that she could not tolerate another woman. Steve promised to reform and one of his associates sneered, "His wife put him on probation."

Although it was not her custom to discuss her problems with others, her friends saw glimpses of her increasing anxiety during the months preceding her murder. The petite, red-haired woman, always slender, seemed thinner and became ever-busy, rarely sitting still.

What may have sealed the fate of 34-year-old Elana on that night of May 21, 1981, was her decision to confront Steve with her doubts about where their money was going. She could no longer either ignore or deny this problem. Not surprisingly, she underestimated her danger.

It is doubtful that Steve could tolerate questions from his wife about his activities. The ferocity of those 26 stab wounds — inflicted with her own 10-inch carving knife as she lay in bed — went far beyond what would be expected in a simple robbery. The knife was wielded so powerfully that it pierced the bones of her skull as well as the mattress, possibly impaling her. Her spleen, liver, stomach, and heart were pierced. The temporal lobe of her brain was pierced after she was dead. Her attempts to defend herself were shown by the non-fatal wounds on her arms and hands. Even the webbing between her fingers was slashed.

The overwhelming savagery of the attack was significant. Steve's activities were rapidly catching up with him and he might well have felt cornered. It would appear that by penetrating his mask of success, his wife elicited the enormous rage that lay not far beneath the surface of his suave exterior.

Steve's call to police was received in the station at 12:07 a.m. A man screamed, "My wife was just murdered, and they walked in the house, my God please—I'm bleeding. I'm trying to stop the bleeding." A child's voice screamed, "This is his daughter, please hurry. I'm here. I'm Tracy. I'm scared."

At midnight, a neighbor heard a woman's screams that lasted perhaps several minutes, followed by a man's angry voice. The neighbor had a momentary concern, but thought that perhaps the Steinbergs were having a party. Hearing nothing more, she went to bed. Only later did she realize that these were Elana's last moments of life.

Police found no forced entry and no footprints in the wet grass. Three pieces of Elana's underwear were spread neatly on the floor, supposedly from the ransacked bureau. On the other side of the room her jewelry—gold chains, earrings, and a diamond watch— was piled behind the mirror of what appeared to be the man's side of the vanity.

Police theorized that Steve planned to take the jewelry and claim robbery. Perhaps it was to be a simple fake burglary, but Elana woke up, protested, and was then attacked. However, from the beginning, police believed the argument that led to murder had already taken place. And, desperate for money as always, Steve's plan was to use the jewelry for an insurance claim after he killed his wife.

Blood from the bed, where the attack took place, still dripped onto the white carpeted floor. Evidence showed that Elana tried to sit up and escape but that she bled to death before she could get away. Her body then slid off the bed. She was found slumped in a sitting position, on the floor, with one leg twisted awkwardly under her. She was drenched with her own blood. The frail-looking woman with the long, red hair was dead.

Police found the older daughter in her bedroom screaming hysterically into the phone. Her younger sister huddled silently on the bed. Barefoot and in a brown robe, Steve walked about the house and yard. He was weeping intermittently and his hand was wrapped in a towel. To family, neighbors, and police he made frequent complaints about the pain in his hand. His cut was found to be superficial.

Officers noted something they described as "off-key" about Steve. When Elana's mother asked him where he was when "they" were killing her daughter, Steve turned away from her. When Steve could not look Elana's parents in the eye, Elana's father first suspected that Steve was the killer. Elana's brother always remembered Steve's odd comment about that night, "There goes 15 years down the drain." At 5 a.m. he was taken to the police station and put into a cell. The fork that matched the murder weapon was found neatly placed in Elana's kitchen drawer, 60 feet from the bedroom.

During the early hours after the murder, Elana's mother simply could not believe that Steve could have killed Elana. Steve had lost his own father early in life and Elana's parents had taken Steve into their home almost as another son when he and Elana met during their teens. Even though they had known Steve since high school, they never suspected that he was a liar and a thief.

What tripped up his habitual aura of success was his uncontrolled spending and long-standing gambling. He was indeed a liar and a thief, but he was so clever, persuasive, and secretive about his activities that he avoided detection. He was able to stage fake robberies to collect insurance and even to rob his in-laws' restaurant safe at least twice. In fact, a rash of robberies seemed to follow Steve wherever he went.

Police had been called to the restaurant six times within two years. Employees viewed these robberies as a kind of joke but did not know who to suspect. To help solve the mystery, Steve insisted that the employees take polygraph tests, but all tests were negative. Steve did not take the test.

After the murder, the pieces of Steve's life prior to the murder began to take further shape. The failing restaurant had been taken over by eastern investors and the new management did not want Steve to stay on. The new owners were aware of the loans he had taken out to pay gambling debts his wife did not know about. They knew that the restaurant safe had been looted. No matter how he appeared, he was not the typical suburban husband.

Shortly before his wife's murder, Steve began taking real estate courses. He continued on, cocky and optimistic as always, and Elana expressed confidence that he would find a new job. At about this time his creditors began pressing for payment. This was a new experience for Steve who had always been able to lie or borrow his way out of life's realities. The facade of a successful businessman was beginning to fall apart.

At the beginning of the marriage, Elana had been unperturbed by her husband's gambling. It was not until a vacation trip to Las Vegas that he lost so much that he had to hide the debt from his wife. His friends all thought Steve a big winner, and they had no knowledge of the direction he was heading. Whenever there was a win he gave his wife one-hundred-dollar bills and jewelry.

Steve needed money for the move to Arizona and borrowed five thousand dollars from his father-in-law. Elana and the girls flew out first and Steve planned to follow in his car. He told his wife he would hire someone to drive Elana's car to Arizona. Late one night in Arizona, Elana received a call from an unknown, harsh-voiced man who said, "Lady, your car just blew up. I'm leaving it here."

When Elana frantically telephoned Steve, who was still in Chicago, he reassured her that there must be some mistake. He would take care of it. No need to worry. When Steve finally went to Las Vegas to retrieve the car, he came home without it. He said that the car was demolished and he would sue those who were responsible. That was the last Elana ever heard about her car. Steve had sold it.

Before the couple ever left Chicago there had been a theft. Steve was alone at home one day when, he claimed, bushy-haired burglars broke into the apartment and tied him up. Although burglaries were rare in this area, the insurance company paid the claim without question.

In Phoenix, a robbery occurred on a fourth of July weekend while Steve was in the restaurant. He claimed that he was held up at gunpoint and that a shot was fired through the watercooler before the robber roared away. Police found a .38-calibre slug in the wall. The cash lost was $7,360. Not until after Elana's murder did anyone, including the police, suspect Steve.

When four thousand dollars disappeared from the cash register, Steve blamed the bookkeeper, although the last person in the store was Steve. The partners who now hold ownership suspected Steve, but his father-in-law defended him staunchly, a fact which caused permanent damage to the relationship between the partners and Elana's father.

Elana's mother entered the hospital for cardiac bypass surgery.

While the family visited her, a burglary occurred in their home. The only sign of forced entry was a tiny window open in the bathroom. It was considered too small to pass through. Of course, the older couple could not, at that time, suspect their own son-in-law — someone for whom they had done so much. There had been an earlier theft of money out of Elana's mother's cookie jar. It was only a couple of hundred dollars, but it was upsetting that someone had entered the apartment. Steve said to her about the supposed unknown intruder, "That dog, he took your money."

By 1979, Steve began to resort to bank loans to pay off gambling debts. He had previously made a bank transaction on Elana's car without her knowledge. Now he obtained loans from at least four different Phoenix banks without difficulty. The Steinbergs' credit was good. Elana always took Steve's paycheck at his request because she was so good at managing money. All bills were paid on time. Elana held two bank certificates of deposit (although one was found to be missing after her death).

The restaurant was filled with customers each day, and, in fact, the loans were often obtained under the pretense that he was a partner in the restaurant and needed loans for expansion. Sometimes, there was no need to give any reason at all. To all the loan applications, without her knowledge, Steve signed Elana's name.

Also in 1979, he had a big win at Las Vegas. To celebrate his success, he gave Elana a new white Cadillac with her initials painted on the side.

After a vacation trip to Coronado Island in San Diego, Elana's watch with a diamond wristband was missing. Steve told Elana she must have not snapped the band tightly. After a Lake Tahoe trip, Steve reported a burglary of their hotel room and a loss of his wife's jewelry. He received an insurance payment of $1,700 for the watch and the jewelry.

He went gambling with his brother-in-law. After the brother-in-law went to bed he was called by the hotel pit boss who said Steve had signed the brother-in-law's name to $9,000 worth of vouchers. After the two men returned home, Steve's brother-in-law told his sister that she should divorce Steve. Elana hung up the telephone.

Steve lost more money; $1,200 disappeared on a trip to Reno,

Nevada. Friends witnessed the Steinbergs' first public argument about Steve's gambling.

The day of the murder was Wednesday, May 27. The weather was overcast. Reconstructing the Steinbergs' day provided no more than a sketchy outline of their activities. The morning paper arrived, and on the front page of one section was the story of the Jeffrey Mac-Donald case. The Supreme Court was taking up the appeal of the Green Beret doctor. The story described long-haired intruders entering his home and murdering his wife and daughters. Elana placed the newspaper on the coffee table in the den.

May 27th was also the day Steve picked up his first unemployment check. In the evening, Elana took one of their daughters to a school concert, using her mother's car, and Steve took the other child to his softball game. In hindsight, Steve was described as being vague and preoccupied that evening. He made an uncharacteristic error on the field.

Later, at home, the girls went to their room. The younger daughter erased pencil marks in her school books that were to be returned next day. Steve received a call from his stepbrother about a loan the brother had given Steve several years earlier, and Elana wondered why his brother was calling now. Elana went to bed and picked up the phone to tell her mother she was home. Steve remained in the study, brooding about the call and watching late-night television. Outside, the rain had begun.

At the murder trial, the jurors believed personable Steve's explanation that his wife's extravagance drove him to temporary insanity. Many of them empathized entirely with the predicament he portrayed: a nagging, spendthrift wife who drove her husband crazy with her bills. It was also testified that his wife called him at work. Each day, Steve wore one of two inexpensive suits which were bought just for the trial. His own clothes were expensive, colorful, and hardly suitable for court. Speaking to his lawyers, he blamed the expensive wardrobe entirely on Elana—drawers of silk shirts had been found. At the trial, when testimony turned toward Elana's extravagance, jurors could note from Steve's drab attire that she certainly did not spend money on her husband.

The bushy-haired intruder story had long since been cast aside. Steve went into the trial as the accused perpetrator of the crime, but attention was quickly diverted to Elana as the guilty party. She was responsible for her own murder. The courtroom testimony against her was a relentless litany of Elana's failings as a wife and mother. The campaign against Elana was so successful that a juror later expressed this opinion: "It was just so clear. The guy shouldn't have been on trial. He should have had a medal."

Elana's friend later said,

> I didn't know Elana was going to need witnesses. Nobody told us that. I feel bad about it now and I think — did I say things that sounded that way about Elana? I didn't mean to do that. I loved Elana.

At first, Steve's friends believed him to be innocent and felt bad for him that he was in that terrible jail cell. Steve called them often from jail and his attorneys held neighborhood meetings to find those who might make good defense witnesses.

Steve wept often in court and behaved as an injured victim of circumstance. Because his lawyers had buttressed their arguments with Elana's demanding greediness, Steve was able to take the high-minded approach with his testimony. He said he did not want to keep putting Elana down. They had a lot of fun. They never argued once they left home (implying that his wife might have given him some difficulty at home, but he did not want to talk about that in court). She was a good mother. She kept a beautiful home. He said that he didn't know he was unhappy or that anything was wrong. They never discussed things, but if she were here today maybe they could talk.

He cried when he spoke of the intruders that he thought he saw that night and he professed amnesia about the killing because of his psychiatrically documented "dissociative reaction." Steve was even able to convince the jurors that Elana's wounds were accidental and superficial.

Steve continued, saying that he did not want to admit the depth of his financial debts because of his pride. Loans were coming due and he had no money. On the day of Elana's death he had to ask his wife for five dollars for gas, but only put in three dollar's worth because he had to make phone calls about the bank loans. The jurors could understand how humiliating that must have been. He talked about his loving mother, how good their relationship had always been. He loved her and was grateful for her nurturance. Again, he wept.

His defense of temporary insanity was successful.

Steve never convinced his daughters of his innocence, although he tried hard to bring them in on his side of the case. The twelve-year-old and her younger sister refused to see him or talk to him ever again. He dropped the custody fight.

Steve walked out of the trial a free man and in possession of his victim's property: the house (which financed his case), her jewelry, and several small life insurance policies. After his acquittal, he quickly shed the inexpensive, conservative business suit that he had acquired to project a demeanor of dignity and respect.

Claus Von Bulow

Claus Von Bulow is a handsome and urbane man-about-town who currently lives in London. His daughter, Cosima, continues to support his innocence.

Although his original conviction of attempted murder was appealed and reversed, as will be discussed, he has renounced his share of Sunny's 100-million-dollar fortune. As of this writing, he has yet to divorce her as he had promised. His female companion is not the same woman whose testimony became a significant part of the first Von Bulow trial.

In retrospect, risk factors for wife murder existed in this widely known case. To date there are two books describing Claus Von Bulow's personality and behavior during his marriage to Sunny. One was written by an investigative journalist (Wright, 1983), and the other by one of his lawyers for the appeal after the first trial and for the second trial (Dershowitz, 1986). Court testimony and extensive interviews with Von Bulow provide information on the potential danger for Sunny.

The most significant warning signal for Von Bulow's original conviction was the alleged failed murder attempt that was made almost exactly one year prior to the similar second incident. It was the second episode that placed her in an irreversible coma.

Claus was known for being coolly poised and in control of his emotions, whatever the situation. Always, both before and after his wife's permanent coma, he conversed easily on many topics. As a European, he was knowledgeable about European history, castles, lineage, economics, and finance. Even during the crisis of his second trial his lawyer found him witty and amusing. He was always willing to digress from the problem at hand to his favorite topics which included social gossip (of which he was particularly fond).

If not for the suspicions of Sunny's children, Ala and Alex, and their steadfast persistence derived from loyalty to their mother, Claus would not have been accused of trying to murder his wife. Whispered suspicions would have remained limited to the local social gossip of their Newport neighbors.

Claus turned Ala and Alex's dogged, unrelenting pursuit of justice into accusations against Sunny's children. He hinted to others about their greed over their mother's estate. Sunny's will divided the 100-million-dollar fortune almost equally between each of the four heirs, Claus and three children. If he were to be eliminated from the heirs, he complained, the pie would be divided into fewer pieces, thereby giving Alex and Ala a larger share of the fortune. However, there is no indication that the children were anxious to receive their inheritance. In any case, their inheritances from their grandmother would far exceed what they would receive from Sunny.

The apparent murder motive for Claus was money, or rather, more money. Sunny had set up a two-million-dollar trust fund from which he was to receive income whether or not the marriage continued. To assuage his growing restlessness, her desire was to make him more independent. Her New York banker supported the request of Sunny and Claus's request for the trust. He stated, at Claus's first trial, that he did so partly to prevent what he feared could happen to Sunny if he didn't!

Von Bulow could not have divorced Sunny without losing his inheritance. The $120,000 per year trust fund income was far from adequate compared with his inheritance. Possibly he figured the wait was excessively long. Sunny was still a young woman.

When Sunny lapsed into a coma, Claus struggled tirelessly and unsuccessfully to persuade Ala and Alex to agree to disconnect her life support system, first in the Boston hospital to which she was first admitted and later at New York's Columbia-Presbyterian Hospital. (When life support finally was disconnected, Sunny did not die and she remains today in an insulin-induced coma.)

Another motive that may have contributed to attempted wife murder was Claus's affair with a woman of status and wealth, also mother of a son by her former husband. She wanted marriage, not a clandestine extra-marital liaison, and she made it clear that she would have a marriage or she would end the relationship. At the first trial she told her story. It was obvious that she had no idea of the enormity of the consequences of her requirement, that it might endanger Sunny's life.

Claus's character was displayed years before the alleged murder attempt. He camouflaged his own shortcomings, notably his greed, on a continuing basis by diverting attention onto misrepresentations about his wife's character. A steady pattern of blaming Sunny emerged. To her family and friends he spoke in ways designed to destroy her reputation, always cleverly doing so under the guise of trying to help her.

Sunny's family, and at least several friends, saw disturbing elements in the marriage, but it is doubtful that any suspected the final denouement. Perhaps divorce, yes, but murder would likely have seemed impossible. They did not share their concerns about Claus with Sunny.

Claus's European background was elusive. Bulow was the original family name before it was changed to Von Bulow. His grandfather was Denmark's Minister of Justice. His father was a playwright and drama critic whose imprisonment for allegedly collaborating with the Nazis during World War II was an embarrassment to Claus.

When Claus was four years old, his parents divorced. He moved to England with his mother where she joined London's social life. Later, Claus attended a Swiss boarding school, meeting affluent boys whose resources far exceeded his own, but he observed and learned. Both mother and son attained social success in London and elsewhere. In the world of haute monde, the conversation swirled around the topics of money, sex, food, wine, the opera, scandals, eccentric dowagers, horses, women, clothes, and jewelry. Claus was a man trained for the life of the salon.

Two facts from in his life before Sunny were not admitted as evidence in the trial. In England one of his closest friends attempted to murder his wife with a lead pipe. Also, during his law studies he learned of a case from the 1950s in which a husband killed his wife by injecting her with insulin.

Claus seemed the perfect companion in the setting of a Fifth Avenue drawing room. His friends said that he would admire beauty, but would marry wealth. At 40 he seemed to have found both. He married Sunny.

Claus was eager for his new wife to use her millions for a high-energy social life. The guests at the parties they attended were his friends, not hers. The blonde heiress often felt awkward, but she tried to join his world as she thought a good wife should. Having entered her second marriage, she wanted to make this one a success. Later her husband would portray her home-loving side, including her interests of reading and swimming in their pool, as evidence of his wife's mental illness.

His employment record was sparse and he was said to overstate his legal training and experience. At the time of his marriage he held a poorly paid position in London with the Getty Corporation. He claimed that, because Sunny preferred to live in New York in her 14-room Fifth Avenue apartment, he had to leave Getty when he married Sunny. Because she would not live in London he complained that he lost possible future advancement opportunities with the Getty company.

Martha, always called Sunny, was the only child of a New York railroad and utilities magnate. Late in life Mr. Crawford married a young woman. Sunny had the distinction of being born in a Pullman car on the way to New York where her mother had planned to give birth in a hospital.

When Sunny was four, her elderly father died. Mother and daughter developed a lifelong closeness that remained throughout her mother's remarriage and Sunny's two marriages.

Sunny graduated from a private preparatory school in New York City. Although bright, she elected not to pursue a college degree. This fact left her with a continuing feeling of inadequacy and lack of self-esteem. She studied on her own and read copiously to remedy what she considered to be her educational deficiency. (After her marriage to Claus, he recommended that she discipline her reading by auditing a course at a local college instead of reading books at random).

Like many wealthy American girls of her time, the young Sunny attended parties in Europe as well as in America. In Europe she met a young, handsome, fun-loving, blonde Austrian count with whom she fell in love. Both her mother and grandmother voiced reservations about the marriage, but Sunny was sure that this was the husband she wanted.

The newly married pair, using Sunny's money, built a large but tasteful home in the Austrian countryside. Several idyllic years followed as well as the arrival of their two children, Ala and Alex, but the paradise could not last. Sunny never really mastered the language, a fact that made evenings with her husband's many friends difficult.

Her first husband's love of sports included car racing, hunting, and other activities which Sunny could not share. And then there were other women, a custom more acceptable in Europe than in America. Finally, Sunny was an American woman who was homesick for her country. The pair parted amicably and continued to be friends. This was a source of annoyance to Claus following his marriage to Sunny.

Earlier, Claus had met Sunny in London and when he learned of the dissolution of her marriage, he hastened to New York to renew the acquaintance. Claus Von Bulow became Sunny's second husband.

When she took him to meet her mother he was wearing a turban around his head because of recent hair transplants. He told Sunny to tell her mother he had been in an auto accident.

After their marriage, Claus set about redecorating the Fifth Avenue apartment and installing an elaborate sound system for his music. A friend commented later, "Usually the new spouse of the one with the money waits a year or two before throwing his weight around."

When a group prepared to tour Sunny's Newport mansion one day, Claus took complete charge. He ignored Sunny to such an obvious extent that the guests were made uncomfortable.

Sunny's friends remained those she had known since her school days and during her first marriage, but Claus found them boring. In their presence the usually relaxed and amusing Claus became arrogant, disinterested, and antagonistic.

Her New York friends found it increasingly difficult to reach her. They found her husband rude. He said she was "out," or "exhausted," or "packing for a trip." Whatever the explanation given as to why they could not speak to Sunny, it was usually given in a way that precluded further communication. Most of them stopped calling. Even Sunny's children, as they grew older and lived away from home, found it difficult to reach their mother.

Claus ordered the family to reduce expenditures and he became aggressively economy-minded. He began going over the checkout receipts at the supermarket. Timers were placed on the lights in the children's closets, 60-watt bulbs were replaced with 40-watt bulbs. When Alex entered Brown University, he earned his own tuition, but Claus talked continually of the children's selfishness and extravagance.

Long-time servants of Sunny's were fired without reason or notice, and without informing Sunny. She could not object. When she discovered that two of her favorite servants were gone, she inquired of their whereabouts. Upon learning that they had been dismissed, she was irate and asked them to return, but somehow they never did.

Sunny's interest in gardening extended to spending many hours with plants and cut flowers, often with the assistance of her maid. When Sunny asked about the paucity of bulbs in the flower garden, which was usually planted lavishly, she learned from the gardener that, for reasons of economy, Claus had reduced the number of plantings. When Sunny discovered that three of her wristwatches were missing, she confronted Claus to retrieve them. Her family described this incident as one of the few times she stood up to her husband. Later, while she was in Austria for her daughter's wedding, Sunny's carefully guarded jewelry box disappeared from her carrying case. At the wedding festivities, Claus was noted to be sullen and cold.

Claus established quick and easy intimacy with others, but telling the truth was never his strong point. The family was aware of this character flaw. When a friend admired a costly item that Sunny had owned before the marriage, Claus was quick to claim that he had given it to his wife as a gift.

His deceptiveness became increasingly significant during the two years before Sunny entered her final coma. Claus embarked on a serious vilification campaign against Sunny, and he extended it to the children from her first marriage as well. He never confronted Sunny and her children directly. Instead, without their knowledge, he connived to feed misinformation to Sunny's friends, doctors, and trust officers. Later, after he was accused of his wife's attempted murder, he fed these same stories to his lawyers and interviewers.

When he entered into a serious relationship with a wealthy and attractive divorcee, she, too, became a target for his deception and manipulation. He dangled the promise that he would divorce his wife.

To his wife, Claus attributed his increasing irritability around the house to his own lack of a career, and he appeared to make some effort in the direction of remedying his unemployed status. He complained to others that Sunny wanted him near her and would not allow him to work. Although he did not say so, divorce was a solution that Claus certainly did not want. Sunny attributed his edginess to his financial dependence on her, and she attempted to assuage his irritability by arranging, through her trust officer, for Claus to receive independent income. Privately, she confided to her son, Alex, that the marriage was not working and she wanted to divorce Claus.

Claus's campaign against Sunny was calculating and wide-ranging. Destroying her self-confidence was part of it. What he said to others about his wife was that nothing he could do made her feel better about herself. He said that he had encouraged her to get her exercise by gardening instead of going to her exercise class and doing so much swimming, but she was resistant. He complained about the lack of discipline in her reading habits.

He also complained that his wife ordered dance dresses and then did not go out to use them. She didn't like his music or the up-to-the-minute sound system he had installed. He whined that she was rich and spoiled. Soon he added the new accusation that she was depressed and drinking too much. An observer might well conclude

that, had she committed suicide, he might have found it a convenient solution for disposing of a wife he no longer wanted.

To Sunny's children he spoke of Sunny's sexual inhibitions since
the birth of Cosima, Claus and Sunny's daughter. Because she was
no longer, according to his story, interested in a sexual relationship,
she had given him license to pursue, in discreet fashion, other female partners. Sunny, he said, was a failure as a wife.

Sunny's mother and grandmother were highly admired women.
Claus denigrated them, calling them the two dominating women in
Sunny's life.

During the two years before the final coma, Claus courted Sunny's
friends whom he had formerly ignored. In strictest confidence he let
it be known that Sunny was depressed and that she was drinking
excessively. Because they thought him a gentleman they could only
assume that the problem was worse than he was willing to say, although they saw no evidence. He spoke to each friend separately,
sharing with each one his concern about his wife's health and telling
each that he did not want the story to get out.

Her maid of 23 years and her children knew that Sunny drank
sparingly. What they did not know at the time was that Claus was
directing the attention of others to her "alcohol problem."

Claus began squiring his wife home early from parties, especially, it seemed, if she appeared to be enjoying herself. The reason, he hinted delicately, was that he wanted her home before she
disgraced herself. Taking her home early might also serve another
purpose. (If she stayed late, it might demonstrate that she drank
next to nothing.) It could also serve a third purpose—that of frustrating and demoralizing his wife. At parties he also began observing her carefully. His behavior indicated to others that his wife required watching.

On one occasion, when old friends came to town, Sunny's friend
planned a dinner party for them and called to extend an invitation to
the Von Bulows. Claus answered the telephone. He lied, saying
that he and his wife would see the friends later in their Fifth Avenue
apartment. Besides, he informed the hostess, he and Sunny never
went out during the week, a surprising response from a man whose
life revolved around social occasions.

Claus informed Sunny's doctor more than once that Sunny was

depressed and had a drinking problem. At a later point he asked her doctor to document this "fact" in writing. He wanted the physician to recommend that Sunny see a psychiatrist. He indicated her need for psychiatric help to others.

There was also the question of drugs. Claus had an interest in various types of drugs, and knew how to inject them. The black bag containing needles and drugs (including insulin) found in his Newport closet was a damning bit of evidence in his first trial. It is considered possible that Claus may have persuaded Sunny to join him in experimenting with one or more recreational drugs. However, no one seriously believed she had a drug problem. There was never any evidence pointing in that direction. During the appeal however, the defense team raised doubts about the black bag, centered on its contents and improprieties in the search of Claus's belongings.

Claus had another balancing act to perform in regard to his mistress. For her it was either marriage or ending their affair. Claus put forth every effort to prevent the loss of his mistress, although he had no intention of divorcing Sunny. What he did was to promise that he would get a divorce but that this was not the proper time to tell his wife. His story was that he wanted to wait until Sunny's health improved.

Claus rented a secret apartment on East 69th Street, and for many months the affair continued with no conclusive plans forthcoming, either for divorce from Sunny or for the promised marriage. Claus continued to live with his wife.

When his mistress complained that he had not separated from Sunny as he had promised, he put the blame squarely on his mistress. Because the mistress had not called him at the time promised, he gave that as a reason he had not separated from his wife.

Finally, his mistress ended the affair and went to Florida. Claus quickly discovered her address and followed her. With his gift of persuasiveness, he succeeded in his mission to bring her back to New York where they resumed their relationship.

As more time passed without progress toward the promised marriage, she began to fear that Sunny suspected Claus of having an affair. She wondered if possibly that could perhaps be the cause of Sunny's continued supposed ill health. The woman had no premonition that something might happen to Sunny, that Claus might be involved, or that she would be called to the witness stand to testify about her affair with Claus Von Bulow.

During 1979-1980, before she entered the irreversible coma, Sunny experienced a coma, a head injury, and finally a second coma. Her life began to close in around her.

Her worried children hesitated to bring up the topic of her marriage, fearing that this would be unacceptable to their mother and hurt their relationship with her. They talked with each other and spoke with Sunny's maid. There seemed to be a problem but nothing anyone could do to help.

The Von Bulows spent the Christmas season at the Newport mansion on Ocean Drive. One morning Sunny did not awaken. Her maid, who had been with Sunny since before her first marriage, was immediately alarmed. When she knocked and entered the master bedroom, Sunny lay motionless. One arm had fallen off the bed and was dangling over the edge of the mattress. Beside her lay Claus, reading a book. He continued to lie calmly beside his unconscious wife all day. He refused to respond to the maid's tearful pleadings that he call the doctor. He talked of Sunny having stayed up too late, having taken a sleeping pill, and sleeping off too much alcohol from the previous evening. The maid could not believe this. She knew Sunny to be a light sleeper.

Not until late afternoon, when Sunny was gasping for breath and there was a gurgling sound in her lungs, was the doctor finally called. The doctor found Sunny vomiting and blue in color. He was unable to get a pulse. She was rushed to Newport Hospital where, on this occasion, her life was saved.

Blood tests showed no barbiturates or alcohol. The low blood sugar was suspected to be the result of an insulin injection, but there was no proof and no wish for additional involvement in the case. It was said that hospital personnel did not want to jeopardize the Von Bulow marriage, however negligent the husband may have been, and the doctor could not see Von Bulow as an attempted murderer. The diagnosis given was bronchial pneumonia.

Claus spoke at length to the doctor about Sunny's problems with alcohol, drugs, and depression. He asked for a letter documenting the problems, including hypoglycemia. He talked about her lack of sexual interest since their daughter's birth and strongly urged the doctor to place his wife in the care of a psychiatrist.

A psychiatrist visited Sunny while she was still in Newport Hospital. She admitted she got depressed sometimes, but doesn't everybody? The psychiatric route was pursued no further and Sunny was discharged from the hospital.

After this first coma, Sunny became apprehensive about going out because of her fear of a recurrence of whatever had caused the mysterious incident. There was talk of low blood sugar and possible hypoglycemia. Claus commented that she ate too many sweets which resulted in instability of her blood sugar level.

Several months later, Sunny's puzzling head injury occurred. The bed sheets were bloody from a head wound. Sunny claimed no recollection, leaving her husband to explain what happened. She became dizzy, tripped, and fell. Her husband said that, when the accident occurred, she was despondent over her daughter Ala's recent miscarriage. Again, the matter was dropped.

At the second trial that freed Claus, the medical examiner for the defense described this episode as the result of an aspirin overdose and probable suicide attempt.

The following Christmas, Sunny's maid of more than 20 years was surprised and hurt when Claus informed her that she would not be accompanying the family on their annual Newport visit that year. He offered no reason.

On the evening of December 19th, 1980, in Newport, the family gathered for the traditional eggnog. Sunny seemed tired and weak, and her voice was almost inaudible. Her son helped her to her room, asking Claus to take care of her, but Claus seemed unconcerned. Alex went out for the evening. The next morning Claus came down early for breakfast and left his wife still sleeping. At nine o'clock Alex went upstairs.

Sunny was sprawled across the pink marble floor of her bathroom. Her pulse was 36-40 and her body temperature was 81.6 degrees. On that chill winter day the bathroom window was found open.

At the Newport Hospital, Sunny's blood sugar remained low for hours and continued to drop despite massive infusions of sugar. It seemed that insulin was "eating up" the sugar as fast as it was administered.

In court, the Von Bulow defense pushed hard to discredit hospital testing procedures and the resulting conclusions (Baden and Hennessee, 1990). The defense acknowledged bruises found on Sunny's body. Although some conjectured that Claus may have held her down to inject insulin or other drugs, the defense expert maintained that they were not inconsistent with minor bruising associated with resuscitation efforts of the medical team.

Tests showed a small amount of barbiturate and alcohol in the blood, and there was the question of whether the barbiturate had been injected or swallowed, and whether the level might have been higher during the time period before she was discovered. In any case, despite all medical efforts, this time Sunny did not awaken.

When the decision was made to transfer her from Boston to New York to be near her home, Claus falsely told Alex and Ala that the New York hospital was more antagonistic to removal of life support than the Boston Hospital.

With Sunny still alive, although permanently comatose, the fortune could not be divided. Alex, accompanied by a locksmith and by Richard Kuh, made a surprise visit to Newport. Kuh was a former district attorney for the City of New York and currently with a private law firm. They found the black bag containing drugs and needles. More drugs were found in Claus's desk. Alex and Ala hired a lawyer and investigator. The result was that Claus became the murder suspect.

In typical fashion, Claus never confronted the children about the accusation. Nor did he show outrage at being implicated. His calm, cool exterior remained intact. What he did instead was to meet with the bank trust officer to ask how much money it would take to "buy off" the children to get them to drop the investigation. Did they want the Newport house? The New York apartment?

Claus portrayed himself as the victim of a vendetta, a conspiracy by Sunny's family. He expressed the opinion that in times of trouble a family should unite and pull together.

He announced that he was going to New Orleans on business. What he really did was to go to the Bahamas with his mistress.

Von Bulow was found guilty in March, 1982. He then contacted a new lawyer, Alan Dershowitz (1986) who joined the defense team and filed a brief seeking reversal of his client's convictions on two counts of assault with the attempt to murder (the first and second comas). The Rhode Island Supreme Court reversed the convictions, and in June of 1985 at the second trial he was acquitted on both counts.

In seeking the retrial the intent was not to determine guilt or innocence, but rather to determine whether there was sufficient evidence to convict. The reversal of the Von Bulow conviction hinged on several points.

The defense attacked the clandestine search for the black bag of drugs that had so greatly concerned Sunny's maid and her children. The children had hired a private investigator, a former district attorney, for the search. Because the search was private, a search warrant was not required in order to obtain evidence to convict. Questions were raised about tampering with the evidence because items in the black bag were examined and handled. There appeared to be some discrepancy about which drugs were in the bag and which might have been placed in the bag.

Dershowitz was able to obtain the private investigator's personal notes, not a part of the first trial, and these also provided a basis for attack. The notes did not recount the presence of insulin in an early meeting with the children. Also, from the notes, the children's possible financial interest in accusing their stepfather could be introduced because her son had indicated an interest in acquiring Sunny's Newport home, Clarendon Court. The children's motives were impugned and greed was the alleged motive in turning against Claus.

Furthermore, Truman Capote signed an affidavit affirming Sunny's interest and ability in injecting herself with amphetamines, vitamins, and other drugs as well. A credible witness for the source of drugs could not be identified. Other information on Sunny's intolerance for alcohol and alcohol consumption cast doubt on Sunny's habits in this regard.

The defense claimed, too, that the comas were the result of alcohol and barbiturates. The used needle with the insulin residue, which had been found in the black bag was discredited by the claim that if the needle had been used to inject Sunny it would have been wiped clean as it was withdrawn from her body. Also disputed were hospital procedures used to discover what was found in her blood and the insulin readings. The defense managed to cast enough doubt to prevent a guilty verdict.

The jury was not permitted to learn what Claus would inherit if his wife died, nor of Claus's acquaintance with the case in England in which insulin was used as the murder weapon.

Claus did not take the stand despite his attractive appearance because, it was decided, this would permit embarrassing questions about his past, his possible financial motives, his knowledge of injectable drugs as well as damaging information about his personal life. He could also be asked why valium and barbiturates were found in an unusual paste form and as liquids in vials instead of the usual pill form. In the black bag at the time of Alexander's search liquid barbiturate, a local anesthetic, and needles were found. Before Sunny's final coma, her maid had seen yellow paste and insulin. The yellow paste (valium in a form that could be added to food) was found in Claus's desk at the time of the search. More drugs were found in Claus's black briefcase.

Brought out at the second trial were Claus's characteristic household frugality, and affirmation that Sunny was a loving, giving person who spoke daily by phone with her mother. This second trial freed Claus.

"BUT AREN'T THESE CASES RARE?"

The above cases are famous enough to be examined more closely than would ordinarily be possible, but they represent only a few of the many that occur. They illustrate what can and does happen. The emotional abuse that may precede the crime can be as risky as physical assault.

If there are warning signs before the fatal attack, they often go unrecognized or are seen as evidence of her problem — her despondency, depression, and feelings of failure. Women still receive twice as many medical prescriptions for tranquilizers as men.

Most published information about criminal cases focuses on the evidence and pursuit of justice rather than on behavioral risk factors. Exactly what happened before the murder, and during the killing, is at least partly obscured by the fact that in most cases the only witness, the woman, is dead. And there may be much about her husband that is unaware of or denies.

IN THE MALL . . .

Three people are in jail awaiting trial for the murder of 20-year-old Sharon Johnson at the Mall of New Hampshire parking lot on July 28, 1988. The pregnant woman, and mother of one, was forced at knife-point to drive to a secluded area where two men beat and stabbed her to death while her husband watched.

The husband was blocked, in court, from cashing in a $100,000 life insurance policy on Sharon, but he was able to collect $50,000 in pension funds from her former employer. Kenneth Johnson, 38, paid $5,000 to each of the two men who killed his wife. All three were arrested on November 28, 1989.

IN THE PARK . . .

In another case, a Berkeley student, Roberta Lee, went jogging one Sunday with her boyfriend in a park near San Francisco. She was missing for five weeks before she was found dead, and all the while her boyfriend joined the search.

Her battered body lay in a shallow grave covered with leaves. There was a large hole in her skull, and by the time she was found a vine was growing out of her stomach. Bradley Page, her boyfriend, confessed and then recanted. Finally, on April 28th, 1988, he was convicted of manslaughter, indicating, according to court information, that there was reasonable provocation and intent to kill but without malice. He would serve a prison term of six years or less. By the time of his conviction he was married and the father of a small child.

In the book written on this case (Thernstom, 1990) the character of Bradley Page remains unclear. Apparently Roberta took off on a different path from the other joggers, he became angered, and somehow there was a fatal attack. No more can be discovered. Perhaps there were no previous warning signs that anyone could have detected.

AT HOME . . .

Lest the Stuart and Marshall cases be considered unique, the Telisnore case in Cambridge, Massachusetts, is alleged to be an insurance case in which the wife was seen as more valuable dead than alive. Her bus driver husband is charged with killing his wife of five months and then setting fire to the house. Her two sons also died in the flames.

The husband is the beneficiary of his wife's $250,000 life insurance policy purchased eight months prior to her death. Because of her accidental death, the double indemnity clause in the contract would apply. However, the bank holding the policy refuses to pay the benefit because the husband is the suspect in his wife's murder (*Boston Globe*, Feb. 2, 1990).

This case may trigger legislative changes that would require that a woman be informed when her husband takes out insurance on her life. The current legislative effort involves requiring a third party to be present to avoid forgery (as in the New Jersey Marshall case). This would also prevent the beneficiary from secretly being changed on the husband's policy (i.e., from his wife to his secretary).

In the Stuart case, Charles avoided suspicion by taking out several smaller policies on Carol's life.

Chapter Seven

"He's Not All Bad": The Cycle of Violence

Even when women are attacked physically, berated, and their property smashed, many remain unaware that they are being abused. Even when he says, "I'm going to kill you," women—for many reasons—regularly deny abuse. They do not see themselves, or want to see themselves as "abused."

Women experience insults and injuries as happening because of something they did, or did not do, and therefore something they can change. Some, whether highly educated or disadvantaged, do not know the language of abuse and assault. Others describe his "temper." They feel unworthy, ugly, and somehow at fault for the tirades and the attacks, even when they have been choked, slashed, or hit.

The dangerous man is only too happy to corroborate his partner's self-blame, especially when she becomes even more compliant and loving in her efforts to avoid humiliating punishment. Furthermore, she redoubles her efforts to make the marriage work, taking even more responsibility for the problem.

Even if she is "only" bruised, her life is at risk. If he raises his closed fist or open hand to her—whether or not he strikes her—it is a warning sign.

Marital rape is a risk factor for injury or death. In addition to rape attacks, in some states there is still sanction for a husband who has found his wife in bed with another man to murder them both. Men have long had the right to protect or avenge the usurping of their property as they see fit. Only now are the laws and the punishment changing. The reverse is never true.

Could she really have married the man who may murder her? "I love him." "We have lots of good times together." And even the incredible, "The children need a father!" She says, "It only happened once under stress."

He may be grouchy, sullen, insulting, and physically dangerous. But, for many, physical strength and force remain associated with maleness, and he is often forgiven aggressive behavior that would not be tolerated in her. Assault, say many, is the weapon of male supremacy. Physical violence places the man squarely in control of the relationship, the family, and the home. The man is almost always stronger than the woman. Why does he resort to violence? The answer experts give is, "It works."

At other times, the marriage seems to be working and she says hopefully, "He says he's sorry." "I can manage." "Things will get better." But they won't, and they don't.

Diane Whitmore Pikul was a 44-year-old Mount Holyoke College graduate whose job was assistant to the publisher of *Harper's* magazine. Her husband Joseph was a successful Wall Street securities analyst.

At work, Diane received frightening phone calls. At home, there were "fights." In her desk drawer she kept an envelope of cash marked "Emergency." In October, 1987, Diane's strangled body was found dumped in an upstate New York culvert. She was murdered in their Long Island vacation home and her body stuffed in the back of the family station wagon amidst camping equipment. Joseph Pikul was arrested, charged, and convicted (Pienciak, 1990).

Charlotte Fedders was among the first women to bring the problem of physical and verbal abuse from husbands to public attention. She was married to John Fedders, the top enforcement attorney for the Securities Fraud Exchange Commission. In 1985, she testified in a Maryland court about the beatings and psychological abuse she endured during the 17-year marriage. She later wrote a book with Laura Elliott (1988) recounting her experiences.

The significant factors associated with male violence have been described in previous pages: strongly sexist attitudes that include expectations of male dominance, controlling men, misogynists, and, harder to assess, the men who are incapable of genuine respect and caring for others, the men "without a conscience." These factors may be interrelated, and all include the possibility of physical and verbal coercion and attack.

Shelters for the emergency protection of women and children were spearheaded by advocates for women needing escape from episodes of male violence in the home. For women's safety in these temporary refuges, only the telephone number can be published.

The connection between assaulted or injured ("battered" is a term many dislike) women and murdered women has been made only in the most tenuous way. Those who work with women (preferably known as survivors rather than victims) do indeed acknowledge that some of these women die, although records are still sparse. And many women who die from husband or partner assaults have never used a shelter or contacted police. Even a known murderer may not be convicted.

Hospital statistics show that at least 20% of emergency room visits for women result from "battering." Violence in the home is the single largest cause of injury to women in the United States. Former Surgeon General C. Everett Koop named domestic violence as the number one health hazard for women in this country (*Boston Herald*, 1991, p. 23). And the figure of at least four wife or partner murders per day is a fact.

For a while, at least, feeling betrayed and bereft, the woman often clings to the illusion of their love—that she loves him, and, of course, that he loves her whatever their problems. The label of "battered woman" often feels like an additional assault on her fragile self-esteem, seeming to place the spotlight on her as the victim instead of on the perpetrator of the crime.

The fact that the verbal abuse and physical violence is unpredictable, that she has no control over its occurrence, produces a situation in the home similar to that of a prisoner of war. Studies have shown that her behavior becomes similar to that of prisoners of war.

Often she can escape only by death, her own or her captor's. Women have stated the problem exactly in these words.

A common characteristic of this man is that he does not leave. If he does leave, he returns. If he also engages in other relationships, he attempts to continue his control over her. And he will not permit her to leave.

Whether he is quiet or in a rage, family members "walk on eggshells," hoping that by discovering and avoiding the "trigger" to his anger they may divert a repetition of the attack. Some men in a relationship with a woman have promised that after marriage she will not have to worry about anything happening again. Not true. His behavior is not generally triggered by women's behavior, although both men and women often mistakenly believe that she has done something to provoke the attack. The problem is his. There is nothing women can do to prevent his periodic eruptions of rage. The harder they try, the more they fall under his domination. Then, when he erupts in anger, the women bear the additional burden of blaming themselves because they failed to avoid the "trigger."

Therefore, it makes little difference that things apparently go back to normal. Family members feel obligated to "forgive and forget," and want to deny, even to themselves, that the assault could ever have happened. The home is, thankfully, once again peaceful, but the problem remains unresolved.

RISK OF REPEAT ASSAULT

Behavior that works is almost certain to be repeated. Statistics show that one attack enormously increases her chance of a subsequent assault. The Bureau of Justice conducted a National Crime Survey from 1978-82. The study found 2.1 million women who had been victimized by husband or partner assault at least once. During the following six-month period, 32% were attacked again. Fifty-seven percent of the assault incidents reported in this study were repeat victims (Bureau of Justice Statistical Special Report, Aug. 1986, p. 3).

Women in these relationships frequently describe the violent man as one who appears out of touch with any emotion except anger. He deals with strong emotions such as alarm, frustration, helplessness, loneliness, jealousy, guilt, insecurity, and feelings of ambivalence in one way: by erupting periodically in sudden rage.

What he fails to show is sustained tenderness, communication, genuine support for family members' needs, joy at their achievements, and a type of caring that allows family members to grow as individuals. This man may be characterized by distance, unresponsiveness, withholding of even the pretense of affection and approval, and giving of orders. Or, he may be on the warpath, ready to attack.

If the woman directs her energy toward convincing him to enter therapy, he may attend one or two sessions "to please her." He blames her for what occurred, trivializes or denies it, and does not change. He makes her feel that she has failed in this effort, too.

If, instead, she seeks professional help for herself to aid her own ability to cope, he may view this development as evidence that the problem is hers. He will be critical of therapy. Unfortunately, due to the focus on her depression and feelings of inadequacy, the power balance between them — already tipped too far in his favor — often becomes still more so. It is also possible for therapy to distance her from the reality of her own danger. Choosing therapy carefully is important, as is described in later pages.

PROMISES, PROMISES . . .

Women's safety demands an understanding of the cyclical nature of violence, whether it be verbal assault, physical attack, or both. After the first assault and his subsequent explanation, if not apology, women can be lulled into a false sense of security.

The *cycle of violence* (Walker, 1980, 1989) has been identified and documented by experts. What is most important, whatever the woman does or does not do, is that she can expect a recurrence. Not only recurrence but escalation is the typical pattern. Only the man can stop what he does, but because violent behavior has provided him with what he wants, he has little incentive to change unless the law or other outside controls intervene to stop him. Walker's cycle of violence has three phases. The *first* is the tension-building phase. The *second* phase is the assault. The *third* is the contrition phase.

As the cycle repeats, the contrition phase becomes shorter and apologies for the assault become few or non-existent. There are fewer pleas for forgiveness and she no longer receives bouquets of flowers. Unless the cycles are interrupted, they tend to become more intense as well as more closely spaced.

The woman in this relationship never knows when the first phase will begin. It may be a time when he is unusually active or moody, more critical than usual, or unusually silent.

During the second phase he experiences a lack of control over his partner. He perceives himself as being "out of control" in terms of what he is doing to her. He justifies his "lack of control" by blaming her. Through violence he re-establishes his control over his partner. Having "won," his tension is relieved, and, if he has driven her away, he exerts every effort to bring her back under his control. He is described as doing everything possible to drive her away, and then doing everything he can to win her back.

The third phase, the phase of contrition, is what binds women to these relationships. For a while they feel loved, and when things go bad again (as they inevitably will), the women hope for the better times that the third stage will bring again. The rage will then be spent and women will be dissuaded from leaving. For the moment, they can relax. However, curiously, even during the third (contrition) phase, this man justifies his furious attack on the bloodied woman. In the case of verbal attacks, the woman is persuaded that she "deserved" them. He avoids taking responsibility. She is his prisoner.

Because he is "nice sometimes," she typically expends great energy trying to prolong the third phase. Unfortunately, she has no idea how long it will last or when he will become tense and primed for another attack. While she seeks to avoid punishment, she may take the problem more seriously if she can recognize that the escalating attacks may one day be fatal.

The woman lives a roller coaster existence. In her attempts to avoid the triggers for possible violence, she becomes more submissive, trying not to provoke his jealousy and trying to appease his anger. She limits her phone calls to family and friends. She avoids disagreements. She does not ask for money.

Her role as mediator between husband and children becomes more important lest the children arouse their father's anger or he becomes jealous of her relationship with the children. With her own spontaneity diminished or absent, her freedom of movement, hobbies, and interests limited, and her association with friends restricted, she lives in the home as though under siege.

Because the outside world sees the public image, not the private behavior, the woman in this relationship can feel very much alone. She is told by family and friends how lucky she is to have such a wonderful husband! If she decides to tell her story, and, unfortunately she often does not, others may find it hard to believe her. Or they assume she "must have done something." "These problems are a two-way street." If she is afraid, her fears are not validated by those in whom she confides.

With increased public awareness, this may change. With outside help she may be more likely to escape her trap.

PREGNANCY AND MALE VIOLENCE

Pregnancy and childbirth have been erroneously considered a time of relative safety from husband assault. At this vulnerable time, a mate's betrayal can be especially devastating. Medical professionals need to be aware of this possibility and take her complaints of depression seriously. Often women attempt to verbalize their distress to their physicians in non-specific ways and their message remains unheard.

Women who have been married for years, with no type of assault from their mates, sometimes experience the first violent incident during pregnancy or the months following childbirth. Whatever reasons are ascribed for his increased aggression at this time, the fact is that, with dangerous men, pregnancy and childbirth become both a time of risk and a time of increased difficulty in leaving the relationship.

Having a child does not "solve" anything. Quite the opposite.

Chapter Eight

"He Lets Me Take Courses": His Control and Her Risk

The controlling behaviors of the men in their lives represent the major existing risk factor to women's safety, as is illustrated in the cases from Chapter Six and elsewhere. The control often appears in so many guises, and has been so socially sanctioned (however inappropriate), that neither the victim nor the perpetrator may recognize the behaviors as abuse! Therefore, a man can often go far out on the control-violence spectrum before experiencing negative consequences. What he commonly says and does is part of the traditional armamentarium of male dominance. Violence and the manipulative mind games of the sociopath may be included.

Women's traditional expectations of playing subordinate roles, together with their accompanying sense of their own inadequacy, may result in their possible victimization. If the answer to a maiden's prayers is a "strong man she can depend on," she may be less certain of her own identity and the appropriate limits of what to accept from others. If she is rescued by her "knight in shining armor" of song and story, to be protected forever after, her understanding of her own rights may become blurred.

If he is the arbiter of truth, where does that leave her judgment? If her statements are routinely prefaced by, "Jim says . . . " then where is she in this picture? If she says, "My husband doesn't eat onions so I never cook them," what is she saying about herself?

If a woman feels that the feminine role includes abdicating much of the family decision making, her expectation is that she will marry a man she can trust. But trust is exactly the issue. When she becomes the victim of a man whose goal is to control her, she may fear him and dread signs of his disapproval, but she cannot trust him.

If a man describes his "strict upbringing" as including parental beatings and being locked in a room, and he vigorously denies that he falls into the category of "abused child," how can he have a clear picture of himself and what drives him today? In his mind, "caring" is equated with "controlling."

If the overly controlling man meets a woman with similar characteristics to those he exhibits, he will label her as a "shrew," "a nag," a "pushy broad," or a "manipulative bitch." He will either feel challenged to attempt a foray designed to coerce and manipulate her into a submissive role, or he will dump her for a more emotionally needy woman whom he can manage.

CONTROL PATTERNS TO AVOID

- If she experiences a relationship with a man as though he were the "father" whom she must obey or face some type of consequence, her feelings of anxiety and intimidation reflect the loss of her adult autonomy. If he becomes angry or ridiculing when she asserts her own opinion or makes a decision, however minor, this is a warning sign.

- If she experiences the relationship with the man "as though I had another child in the house," and if she caters to his needs in this context, she becomes the "mother." She feels responsible for meeting all his needs, whether coping with his demands as in the case of a "spoiled" child, soothing his anger and jealousy, or keeping track of what he needs to do. She feels responsible for him, not as a friend and lover, not as a husband or another adult, but as a needy and helpless child. If she has a child, she feels caught in the middle of a "sandwich." Because he is also an adult who feels entitled to enforce compliance with his demands, his partner is at risk of victimization.

- In any relationship, both man and woman expect emotional support from their partners. However, if the relationship feels permanently lopsided or uncomfortable, instead of feeling guilty about their own fatigue and inability to cope, women should step back to take note.

• If the two cannot talk, for whatever reason, there is a problem. Beyond the normal communication breakdowns that occur at times, if the two cannot listen to each other, discuss problems, consult with each other on areas of individual expertise, and genuinely respect each other's point of view, there is no way to resolve conflicts.

• If he regularly talks "at" her instead of "with" her, or if he withdraws from all discussions of differences, there is no outlet to relieve anger. While she may become depressed, his response may be to strike out verbally or physically, or both, to overpower and punish her. The purpose is to restore what he perceives as an unbearably frustrating loss of control over his wife and family.

All of these illustrate disregard for the woman as a person apart from the functions she performs, whether he leaves her, attacks her verbally, injures her, or kills her.

HER MIND, HER BODY, HER MONEY, HER FREEDOM, HER LIFE

Gelles and Straus (1988) state, in their book, that the family is society's most violent institution, with the exception of the military in time of war. They describe the marriage license as a license for violence that would not be tolerated among strangers, and one made possible only by the inequality of the sexes.

They describe enabling factors such as lack of controls on child spanking, the number of unwanted children, and the long-standing indifference of physicians and the public to what occurs within the home. The costs of violence to society far exceed the punishment for violence at home, and women who are dependent on male favor have been the victims.

In March of 1989, Lisa Bianco and her mother were hiding in a small cottage in Indiana, fugitives from Lisa's violent ex-husband. When she pressed charges against him, he threatened to kill her. He

was jailed, but was later furloughed on an eight-hour pass. Through
an unexplained error in the system, Lisa and her mother were not
notified. After learning where Lisa was staying, he headed straight
for the cottage.

They heard the sound of breaking glass. Lisa's ex-husband entered the cottage through the back door. She had just stepped out of
the bathtub. She managed to escape out the front door, running in a
direction away from the children as she had been directed to do in
case of emergency. He chased her across the street. At the neighbor's front door he caught her, spun her around, and killed her by
slamming a gun barrel against her head (*The New York Times*, Mar.
12, 1989).

"NOBODY'S PERFECT": THE CONTROLLING BEHAVIORS CHECKLIST

Conflict resolution is not always ideal, but sometimes it is impossible. The result may run the gamut from loss of hope, depression,
and anger to emotional pain, physical injury, or death. The violence
continuum ranges from emotional coercion to verbal threats, physical force without a weapon, and using a weapon.

"You Must Be Crazy to Think I'd Let You Go"

The most significant controlling behavior is refusal to "let" her
leave, separate, or divorce him. He takes the car keys and the
money. He threatens her in all manner of ways. By leaving the
home she may become vulnerable to losing both the house and custody of the children because "she left." The physically violent man
would often rather kill her and die himself than separate from his
wife.

He squirrels away money and threatens to ruin his business so
there won't be any child support or mortgage money. He demeans
her. He attacks her reputation. He will not go through with a divorce that does not give him sole custody of the children. He keeps
her in court continually, for one reason or another. He tries to woo
her back. He demands sexual favors in return for her court-ordered
child support money. He parks outside her house. He uses child

visitation rights to harass her. He violates court restraining orders that were issued to keep him away from her.

All of the above are only too common. In fact, they can almost be expected.

Other behaviors that occur before, during, and after the marriage and that may characterize a controlling man are:

- using any type of physical coercion
- destroying property
- being cruel to animals
- showing an explosive "temper"
- slamming doors
- intimidating or bullying weaker family members with loud voice, gestures, intimidating looks
- maintaining constant, critical watch on his spouse
- keeping her "off balance," not knowing what to expect regarding his moods
- using male privilege to treat her like a servant
- claiming to be "the authority"
- using "logic" to undermine her opinions
- telling her she is a stupid, crazy, hysterical woman who needs a psychiatrist
- interrupting her conversations, changing topics, not responding, twisting her words, manipulating the children
- pressuring her to make decisions quickly
- making all the "big" decisions, blaming her for all unsatisfactory outcomes, and telling her the children's problems are her fault
- being cold and withholding
- lying, withholding information
- interfering with her sleep
- interfering with her job, sabotaging her job
- trivializing her complaints

- using ridicule or sarcasm to "put her down"
- abusing drugs or alcohol
- being obsessed with her, refusing to accept separation or divorce
- being jealous of her, her friends, her family, the children
- being unfaithful
- accusing her of infidelity
- telling her she is ugly, unappealing, does not attract him sexually
- forcing sexual intercourse, including sexual acts with which she is uncomfortable
- forcing her to watch pornographic videos, demeaning her if she refuses
- preventing her from becoming economically independent
- insisting on selecting her clothes, especially for occasions important to him
- criticizing her taste and appearance
- isolating her from family and friends
- reneging on shared responsibility, not picking up after self, insisting on spreading his things throughout the house
- criticizing her cooking and housekeeping
- refusing to bathe or shave
- ignoring and neglecting her
- denigrating his family of origin, not maintaining family relationships
- denigrating her family members
- withholding help from children for their homework
- accusing her of neglecting the children
- threatening to take the children and the house and to commit suicide if she leaves
- withholding money, spending excessively on himself, using

her money as he sees fit, not wanting her to have her own
money
   • making her afraid to leave him

Having guns in the home may increase her risk of being killed.

CAN THIS BE SEXUAL ABUSE?

The above checklist contains several factors that are not commonly identified with sexual abuse because they occur in a marriage
or partner relationship. For years, controversy swirled around the
question of whether marital rape could actually exist because of a
man's "conjugal rights." In 1976, Nebraska became the first state
to abolish exemption from the law for marital rape.

Forced sex; requiring her to perform sexual acts she does not like;
waking her to meet his sexual demands; forcing her to watch pornography that victimizes women; ignoring her sexually; telling her
she is fat, ugly, and unappealing; accusing her of infidelity; being
unfaithful to her—all are indeed defined as sexual abuse.

Control, not sexual pleasure, has long been known as the most
significant factor in rape. The goal of rape is to dominate and humiliate the victim using sex as the weapon. Women's danger from
forced sex can be great because rape and murder are often combined.

Sexual abuse by husbands or partners is a risk factor endangering
women's lives.

"THE PLYMOUTH MURDERS"

In a 1990 Massachusetts case (*Cape Cod Times*, Mar. 5, 1991),
Donna Dunn attempted to divorce her husband. Her mother had
come from Alabama to be with her daughter. In the kitchen of the
Dunn home, both women were shot twice in the head.

The killer was dropped off at the Thatcher Road home. After the
shootings, he drove away in Donna's blue Lincoln car. The abandoned car was found near Cape Cod's Sagamore Bridge.

According to adult children in the family, Donna's murder was preceded by years of physical and verbal abuse, including verbal abuse of the entire family.

For lack of evidence, Donna's husband has not yet been charged, and the children have offered a $10,000 reward for information about the murders. The younger daughter still lives with her father.

Because Donna was unable to carry through with the divorce, her husband stands to inherit her considerable estate. If she had been able to obtain her divorce, he might also have had to share his assets, many of which are claimed to have been hidden. Furthermore, his business affairs might have come under scrutiny.

Generally suspected, although as yet unproven, is that Donna's husband was unwilling to let his wife leave their marriage alive.

Chapter Nine

The Dangerous
Green-Eyed Monster

Jealousy is so commonly mistaken for evidence of love that it requires highlighting. Jealousy represents a major risk factor for women with controlling husbands or partners, and it may flare in response to almost anything she likes or does. Husbandly revenge in response to perceived, or actual, rivals for a wife's affections has frequently been legitimized as a reason for murder. The following illustrative cases, with the ascribed motive of jealousy, are far from rare.

THE VALENTINE'S DAY MURDER

The prosecutor's opening statement included the words, "The base human emotions of jealousy, anger, and resentment were catalysts leading to this tragic murder." The defense lawyer for Jimmy Sheriff pled insanity.

This was the case of the woman obstetrician (Chapter One) stabbed to death in bed at their apartment in Waltham, Massachusetts. It happened on Valentine's Day, 1987. Her husband was found unconscious beside the bed; he having apparently tried to commit suicide by ingesting pills.

Jimmy was an unemployed electrician who suspected his wife of having an affair. In the days before the stabbing, Jimmy confronted his wife at the hospital, and on several occasions he had harassed her co-workers.

THE "BURNING BED ATTACK"

This 1990 incident was given its name because of an earlier television movie based on the book of the same name (McNulty, 1989) that pioneered the publicizing of the terrors of male battering.

In Ashland, Massachusetts, James Mitchell, 57, was charged with mayhem as well as assault and battery with attempt to murder (and the burning of a dwelling). He is alleged to have poured gasoline on a 49-year-old woman friend and set her afire in bed. She then ran to a neighbor's house from which she was taken to a hospital intensive care unit for treatment. She was found to have burns over 40% of her body.

Before setting her afire, Mitchell accused her of seeing another man. Two days after the attack, he turned himself in. He was treated for a burned hand and ingesting some type of medication.

RETRIEVING HER BELONGINGS, LOSING HER LIFE

Richard Simmons murdered his estranged wife, Denise, 26, on September 5, 1989. He stabbed her 11 times, twice in the back, when she returned to the apartment she had once shared with her husband to retrieve her clothes. It happened on the day she had started a new job with an insurance company.

Richard attempted to conceal the crime by changing his clothes, washing off Denise's blood and stabbing himself twice superficially. He was convicted of first-degree murder.

After a stormy relationship and shortly before her death, Denise had filed for divorce. Richard's jealousy was aroused because she was seeing another man (*Middlesex News*, Aug. 25, 1990).

"THE MOST POPULAR GIRL IN TOWN"

Early one Sunday morning, Beth Buegge was found fully clothed, slumped in her red convertible outside a restaurant. There was no blood. She was dead, strangled with two bare hands.

It happened during the summer of 1990 in Milwaukee, Wisconsin. Her family is offering a $5,000 reward for information. The suspected murderer is her boyfriend. He was taken into custody after the crime, but no confirming evidence has been discovered.

Beth is described as a nice person, easygoing and generous, with a happy, outgoing personality. At her funeral, five former boyfriends carried her casket, but from her current boyfriend, Beth's family received no acknowledgement or condolences.

She had spent Saturday night with her boyfriend at his home. His story is that Beth left early on Sunday morning before his mother awoke. He has nothing more to say.

Preceding the murder, Beth had done an outdoor photo layout. The scene was photographed on a dock with Beth in a white swimsuit. It was her first foray into modeling. The photographer later described her nervousness about accepting the job. She said her boyfriend would be jealous because the swimsuit was too "revealing." But then she decided that she was 21 and could do what she wanted. The pictures were taken.

She died only days later. She never saw the completed photo layout.

ANOTHER BODY IN THE TRUNK

In Maine, during 1990, when Jerome Howard learned that his estranged wife Joan was seeing another man, he paid her a visit. She was staying in the home of a woman friend.

Howard was known as a quiet, diligent machinist. He and Joan had known each other for years. The two had attended high school together in the picturesque seacoast town of Waldoboro.

Howard stabbed her to death, stuffed her body in his car trunk, and drove to Boston where he then shot himself. Their 11-year-old son was orphaned (*Boston Globe*, Jan. 25, 1990).

OTHER CASES, OTHER PLACES . . .

During the 1980s, Dorothy Stratton, a centerfold model for Playboy Magazine, was murdered by her jealous ex-husband who then shot himself.

Also portrayed in a 1991 television movie was the case of the former model, Marla Hanson. She rejected a would-be suitor who then slashed her face to destroy her career. Her publicized courageous comeback has led her to the profession of directing instead of modeling.

Chapter Ten

Will He Change?

The 1981 study funded by the Minneapolis Police Foundation found mandatory arrest to be the most effective police response for reducing further violence. This places the arrest requirement on the police (as in any other crime).

If nothing more than allowing the husband to "cool off" is done when police come to the home, this is no solution for the inevitable, escalating repetition of the violence cycle. If he has access to her, there is nothing she can do, or not do, to prevent recurrence and possible death. He may stalk her for years. He does not give up.

If she decides not to press charges out of fear or unrealistic hopes that the assault will never happen again, her position is weakened. On the other hand, if she does decide to press charges, she may be in increased danger. The most effective response, that of police responsibility, is slowly becoming mandatory in states across the nation.

State laws should also include arrest for violation of restraining orders that have been issued to keep the man away from his spouse. Women assaulted in dating and non-marital relationships are also beginning to be included.

What women want to know is, "Can he change?" "Will he change?" Arrest interrupts physical violence but does not halt wide-spread abuse that does not involve physical assault.

Although treatment results for men who inflict bodily injury have become available, there is no research focused on treatment of men who verbally assault their wives and partners, who treat them as property to use or discard, and who kill for insurance money or to protect their estates in the event of separation or divorce. Information is only available on men who have been arrested for violence that has progressed to physical attack.

DEBUNKING MYTHS AND MISCONCEPTIONS

David Adams (1988) is one of the few who have studied causes and treatment of men's violence against female partners. Often, in the past, preservation of the marriage has taken priority over women's safety. He zeroes in on common myths.

Adams has followed the problem from the time when fatal attacks on wives were trivialized as a "domestic problem," implying lesser significance than "crime." Based on his clinical experience, he criticizes descriptions of the violent man's as "anger control" problem, helplessness in the face of his explosive impulses, low self-esteem, and lack of (appropriate) assertiveness and verbal skills. Another misconception is that the attacker has brief, irrational episodes that are abnormal enough for him to be considered ill but not responsible enough for him to be considered a criminal.

Apologists for the assaultive man portray him not only as a victim of child abuse but of his wife's verbal and emotional, even physical, abuse. They describe him as a victim of an "impulse disorder." He is not "bad" or "immoral," thereby allowing psychiatric treatment to take place in a "morally neutral setting." Adams disagrees.

Physical assaults are often only one segment of male control used to reinforce verbal directives — threats, intimate coercion, and manipulation are also used to achieve male dominance. If counseling only succeeds in teaching violent men to control women in nonviolent ways, the fundamental problem remains.

Adams addresses and evaluates treatment models frequently used for violent men. The focus may be on childhood factors, alcohol, and feelings of insecurity. Assaults are thereby seen only as a symptom to be dealt with only after resolving insecurity, instead of as the primary problem.

Not every man who is insecure, alcoholic, an adult child of an alcoholic, or the child of an abusive parent, assaults the women in his life. This man does not assault anyone other than his partner. He is selective about how and to whom he is violent in given circumstances. When a policeman arrives at the door he "stops on a dime."

Treatment models that have been used include the following:

1. *The Insight Model,* directed toward understanding the man's low frustration tolerance, fear of intimacy, fear of abandonment, underlying depression and impaired functioning. Emotional deficits resulting from earlier family problems are discussed. The goal is awareness of the past to enable a more appropriate response in the present.

Implicit is the notion that violent men have a fragile sense of self that needs bolstering, but the specific problem of violence against the woman in his life remains unaddressed. His responsibility for change is delayed or avoided. This model does not heed social sanctions encouraging men to develop misogynistic values and controlling behaviors.

A survey of 59 batterer programs found that 90% cited "increased self-esteem" as one of their primary treatment goals. Only 14% listed "having the abuser take responsibility for his violence."

Feminists say that male violence fosters fear, self-blame, and submissiveness in the victim. That is the fundamental reason for violence, whatever emotional problems the man has. The controlling man gains benefits and compliance from his violence. Furthermore, violence against women is eroticized, glamorized, and commercialized.

The case of John "Sledge" Slajinski goes to trial during 1991. One might wonder whether the above treatment model, if recommended, would serve any purpose.

In Denver, Deborah Feiner of South Dakota kept returning to Sledge despite his regularly occurring violence. He even locked her out of their Denver house naked one night. But she wanted to be "loved." He made an X-rated movie of her to help her look "bad" in court. When the two bought a business, he bought it in his name alone. Because John had had a criminal record, he bought the gun that killed Deborah in her name.

2. *The Ventilation Model* is based on the theory that suppression of anger can be the cause of many disorders from ulcers to violence. Honest communication replaces stored-up aggression, and violence toward women is considered to be due to lack of communication. Included is the concept of "fighting fair." There is the mistaken belief that verbal aggression diminishes the likelihood of physical aggression. In this model, the distinction between violent and non-violent clients becomes blurred.

Adams disagrees with the concept of this model. Men do not need expert permission to continue to vent their anger with little regard for its consequences. Angry outbursts become confused with communicating honest feelings. Men's distorted interpretation of their authority allows both partners to avoid confronting men's violence.

Women who have trusted this model in couples therapy have been hurt by it. Women expressing their feelings and opinions in a "safe" environment have been assaulted almost as soon as they left the therapist's office. Women fearing repercussion have expressed themselves indirectly in therapists' offices only to be viewed as being uncooperative in the sessions. To be open with her feelings, however, is to invite grave danger.

3. *The Interaction Model* is similar to the Ventilation Model, but here violence is seen as an interpersonal transaction. The term "battering couples" is even heard, as though the fault is also hers. Yet experts all agree that this is not so. She cannot cause his violence.

Her contributions to the problem—the way she dresses, withholding sex, her angry accusations, her nagging, her failure to adequately state her own needs—are discussed. "His" violence becomes "the" violence. She is given the assignment of helping him bring his anger under control. Virtually any of her behaviors may be deemed "provocative."

Therapists may accept his characterization of his female partner. For example, if a woman continues to negotiate beyond the point where the man has said the argument is over, he reserves the option of labelling her continuing talk as "provocative" or "nagging." Interactive therapists may fail to see her behavior as resulting from his violent control.

4. In the *Cognitive-Behavioral Model,* violence is the primary focus of the treatment. Self-observation is used. He may be asked to keep a journal to monitor his anger. The focus is on understanding his rigid, irrational thought patterns, but he is not challenged to learn flexible and accommodating responses to conflict. Stress reduction is part of this model, as is improvement of his interpersonal skills, but the power and control dimensions of the problem are ignored. There is no explanation of why the woman is his sole target.

THE PROFESSIONAL MODEL OF TREATMENT

Developed by Emerge, Inc. (see Resources), the first counseling group (1977) organized to treat violent men was founded and directed by Adams. This model utilizes up-to-date information methods specifically designed for men who are dangerous to their wives.

It acknowledges the power imbalance and includes verbal as well as physical attack. The withholding of praise has been found to be an especially effective method of controlling women. This undermines the woman, forcing her to strive harder for his approval. He combines this with criticism and physical punishment. This gives him the power to validate her or not.

The sexist belief is that violence is a legitimate way to solve problems, and that it is all right for men to control women. Men's denial of their problem is reinforced by the "conspiracy of silence" on a societal level.

The unacknowledged emotional care-taking men receive from women, says Adams, often enables violent men to maintain a relatively high degree of functioning and competence outside the home. Their inflexible behavior is limited to partners.

The "liberal" man is seen as dangerous to women as well as the "traditional" man. The "liberal" man feels that men are in the same boat as women and rails against "reverse discrimination" toward male nurses and fathers' rights to child custody. He talks about women who "batter" men.

The Emerge treatment model challenges sexist expectations and controlling behaviors. The first response noted of men referred for court-mandated counseling is minimization of violence, use of denial, projecting blame on others, and blaming of stress, drugs, and his "loss of control."

A common initial response to treatment is an attempt to end his wife's doubts about his ability to change. He may issue ultimatums or deadlines for her to make up her mind, accuse her of infidelity or threaten infidelity, use the children as allies against her, and accuse her of not appreciating his attempts to change.

He then resorts to bargaining about how much or how soon he will give up his violence and how many counseling sessions he will attend. He may make cosmetic changes (for appearances only). His changes are dependent on receiving immediate recognition and concessions from his wife.

His conversation typically is characterized by attempts to denigrate and devalue his wife instead of understanding her. Instead of reporting what she actually said, he trivializes or mocks her. "She went on and on about nothing." "She was in a bitchy mood." "There was no pleasing her." "She really knows how to push my buttons." "She exaggerates."

Emerge client findings have been that most abusive husbands lack the internal motivation to enter counseling or change behavior. Approximately 20% of clients are court-ordered to attend. The rest are technically self-referred but are only there because their relationship with their wives will not continue unless they attend. Fifty percent drop out after the first month, a figure that is consistent with other programs. Some drop out as soon as they reconcile with their wives; others drop out as soon as it becomes clear that a reconciliation with their wives is not possible. One third of the clients are professional men. Their perception of the problem is that their wives left them, not that they have been violent. Most have a "quick fix" mentality with a desire to restore the status quo, not to effect change. Gifts may be used to undermine her defenses and to pressure her to return.

Although police are more likely to arrest if substance abuse is involved, the use of alcohol or other drugs does not cause men to assault their wives. Recovering alcoholics are noted to exhibit a high rate of abusive behavior. Therefore, referrals to drug treatment programs alone, without responding to the violence for which he was arrested, will not address the problem.

Extreme possessiveness and jealousy is a significant indicator of homicide.

SUCCESS STORIES

Adams finds that some men do change as a result of counseling and describes the stages of change as those occurring during the grief process. They are denial, anger, bargaining to retain elements of control, depression and confusion (not knowing how to act when they are not in control), and, finally, the acceptance that he cannot control how others act or feel. He also describes those who expect success from counseling alone as naive.

Legal sanctions are essential. Pro-arrest policies must be in place. Counseling must not simply help men circumvent legal consequences of past or continued violence. Arrest, even without conviction, increases women's safety.

Men who make the most significant changes are those who accept legal sanctions and persevere with counseling that focuses on *his* rather than on *her* behavior.

MEN CONFRONTING MEN

Several men's groups, on college campuses and elsewhere, have organized to combat male violence against women. Their message is that any form of abusive behavior is unacceptable. Their major concern is those in society who acquiesce through silence and inactivity.

Men to End Sexual Assault was organized as a project of the Boston Area Rape Crisis Center. In 1990, several groups working to redefine masculinity—Real Men, Organization of Men Against Sexism, and others—presented a week of programs in Boston that called for an end to male violence.

Chapter Eleven

"You Have to Sleep Sometime": Do Women Kill Their Mates?

Pronouncement of the fact that at least four women are killed every day by husbands or sexual partners invariably invokes the bemused response, "But don't women kill, too?"

What is seized on is a "fatal attraction" murder named after the film of that name in which female jealousy and obsession led to violence. In a current "fatal attraction" case, the killer may not have been the man's mistress—perhaps the man hired someone to kill his wife. Or the Jean Harris case in which the 50-year-old headmistress of a private school was sentenced to more than 15 years without parole for fatally shooting the treacherous and manipulative Scarsdale Diet doctor. Still recalled is the Lizzie Borden case, from 150 years ago, in which she was accused of killing her punitive father and stepmother "with forty whacks."

Police called to the home for a "domestic problem" or "lovers' quarrel" have voiced this fear of women's retaliation against male aggression. Arriving at the home they find her afraid to say much in the presence of her husband and the husband acting as though he wonders why the arm of the law is on his doorstep.

When the policeman calls him outside for a chat, to help prevent a recurrence of what apparently happened, the husband may be warned, "You have to sleep sometime." Implied is that the wife may display male-pattern revenge. He had better watch out!

The fear of women rising up against their powerlessness has been illustrated by women's frequent vulnerability to greater punishment than men receive for committing similar crimes. How dare she flout authority and disobey the law? The laws differ in each state, and outcomes are highly dependent on financial resources and the responses of judges, lawyers, and juries.

The gender gap in justice for men and women has been documented by Browne and Williams (1989) and others. One case in which the punishment appeared not to fit the crime took place in 1984. A Duxbury, Massachusetts fireman crept into the bedroom and assaulted his wife, Carol Freeman. The attack resulted in lifelong injuries to Carol, including a severed ear and multiple fractures. The state hospital declared the husband not criminally responsible by virtue of temporary mental illness. He was released and reinstated in his job. However, after a second midnight assault on his wife, he was fired by the town in 1985. In September 1991, the Massachusetts Commission Against Discrimination returned him to his job with $200,000 back pay, including emotional distress and 12% interest (*Boston Herald*, October 11, 1991, p. 1). The town is appealing the decision.

Women's powerlessness has been reflected in the legal response to their attempt to protect their children against their husbands' incestual assaults. There are hundreds of cases, the most famous is the Elizabeth Morgan case (*The New York Times*, Sept. 27, 1989). Morgan, a plastic surgeon, spent nearly two years in a Washington, DC, jail for refusing to divulge the whereabouts of her daughter who was born shortly after the couple separated.

During the uphill legal battle, Dr. Morgan's reputation has been attacked as well as that of her family. The purpose is to divert attention from her husband's problem and to help him obtain custody of his daughter. He is alleged to have sexually abused a daughter of a former marriage and been refused visitation rights as a consequence. Morgan's daughter, also allegedly sexually abused, is in the position of having to visit, and perhaps live with, her accused rapist. Dr. Morgan's husband was never formally charged.

The headline in a Rhode Island newspaper announces, "Batterer Sues Granny for 23K." A 77-year-old Cranston woman, whose son died in Vietnam, was jailed for refusing to divulge the whereabouts of her daughter and granddaughter. For five years she has not seen either of them.

Five years ago, when her daughter discovered her husband on the family boat with another woman, the guilty husband assaulted her. She and her daughter escaped into hiding where they remain. Her husband wants his family returned to him. After a vociferous public outcry, Mary Pidgeon was released "to do community service" (*Boston Globe*, Sept. 12, 1990).

Women do sometimes kill their mates, but almost invariably this occurs in response to years of physical and psychological abuse. They kill because they fear for their lives and the lives of their children.

Approximately 5% of spousal murders are committed by women (Jones, 1980; Walker, 1989), although almost always in self-defense. In 85-90% of these murders, police had been called to the home at least once in the preceding two years (National Woman Abuse Prevention Project, 1990, p. 13).

Because women are generally physically weaker than men and less proficient in physical defense as well as the use of weapons, they can be expected to "lose the fight" in a "family scuffle." They will fight only to defend themselves.

In recognition of this fact, during 1990, over 100 Ohio women who had been imprisoned for killing their husbands had their cases reviewed for pardon from the governor. Only 25 were pardoned, but even this outcome evoked editorial response. The message was that women were given "license to kill" (*USA Today*, Oct. 4, 1990)!

For years, self-defense has been questioned regardless of police visits to the home and the number of times the woman has been treated for injuries from husband assaults (Walker, 1989). Even if she knows he is returning to shoot her, and she prepares to defend herself upon his return, she may be charged with premeditated murder! She may have to prove the "fight" was actually in progress when she finally pulled a knife or grabbed a gun. This almost certainly results in her injury or death. More likely, he is the one given "license to kill."

In a case where the husband died several weeks after his wife had escaped from their violent home, the wife exclaimed, "I'm glad I wasn't there. They would probably have thought I killed him." A combination of amphetamines and alcohol caused this husband's collapse, after which the ten-year-old son (in his father's sole custody) called his destitute mother, saying, "Daddy fell downstairs." In the hospital, the assault victim (the wife) was given the decision about "pulling the plug" on the brain-dead man, the father of her four children.

In general, the reasons men give for killing wives do not apply in reverse. Keeping him subjugated using physical force or weaponry is not the pattern. She does not feel the urge to "slug him" if he asks about her life or challenges her on some issue.

She is unlikely to have the "got to win" mind-set that requires the ultimate annihilation of her opponent. She does not castrate him and leave him bleeding in his bed or the front seat of his car.

Despite comments like, "It takes two to tango," or "She brought it on herself," assault initiated by a wife or female partner is rare. She is more likely to seek a dependent role in the relationship.

Assault of husbands by a wife or female partner is rare whatever he does, whether he plays the passive role of helpless child or the demanding taskmaster, or leaves her bleeding in the front hall.

Women may not be supportive of another woman who kills in self-defense. In a Florida case, the previous wife of an assaultive man said with pride and self-satisfaction, "At least I didn't kill him."

Browne's (1987) research reveals that men are the overwhelming perpetrators (86%) of all homicides in the United States. The majority of female-perpetrated homicides are directed against partners. If men become the victims of female perpetrators, the men were more likely to have first used force or threat, and thus to have precipitated their own death. Almost all women charged with deaths of mates have been victims of assault, usually repeated and incredibly brutal assaults.

"YOU HAVE TO LOVE HIM, NO MATTER WHAT"

Women who kill resort to murder largely because of failure of the legal system to protect them and their children. They are the victims of societal attitudes that seem to say, "You have to love him, no matter what."

Until the 1970s, in some states, a single assault from a husband was inadequate to obtain a divorce. This gives legal support to the attitude that being an assault victim is no reason to break the vows of marriage.

Chapter Twelve

Picking a Partner:
"A Few Good Men"

Women often still express feelings of being incomplete if they are not either in a relationship or married. They have long been socialized to depend on serving others and even living through others—their husbands and children—for their identity. This includes dependence on husbands for economic survival, social standing, and direction in life (see Siegel, 1988). Women have seen themselves as becoming adults by finding a man and getting married. Their families may urge them not to be "too picky."

With these assumptions, the woman, instead of setting realistic limits, therefore has the goal of finding a marriage partner. And if the man pressures her into sex prematurely, into supporting both of them with her job, or whatever else in the name of love, she accepts his definition of what both of them should do. His demands may be prefaced by the words, "if you really loved me . . . "

As a result, many women settle for relationships with men that are far from ideal as well as possibly dangerous. "Why does she stay?" is a common question.

She does not want to "break up the home." "Where would I go? What would I do?" "He'd kill me." "I'm lonesome." "The children need a father." "I can manage." "It's not that bad." "There has never been a divorce in my family." "At my age I may not find another man." "Things will get better." "He is nice sometimes." "I love him." "I need him." "I left him for four years, but I couldn't survive financially. I had to come back." "He's no Prince Charming, but who is?"

Trading the role of victim for survivor is a difficult step to take for women acculturated to be grateful for small favors from men in their lives.

Although men no longer have the right to act violently against wives or people with whom they live, the spirit of the law remains ambivalent. And many women continue to collude unknowingly by being themselves unsure about their own rights and what to accept and expect from others.

He comments negatively on what she eats and where she goes. He is often cold and withholding, insolent, helpless, and demanding. The relationship is "on again, off again" depending on his moods and his terms. His humor centers on women's frailties. Too many women still see all this as just part of "the marriage package."

The man may not hit, knife, or shoot her, but there is danger for women in relationships with controlling, egocentric, possessive, hostile, jealous men. These women live in fear of verbal assault, potential attack, and possible death. Giving the behavior a name helps identify and validate it for what it is.

The Carol and Charles Stuart case, the Von Bulow case, "the woodchipper case," and others in this book do not represent aberrations. They happen every day. In fact, at least four times a day.

Marriage and partner relationships would be better served if women set standards and limits for what they find acceptable. They should make commitments only to men with whom a relationship is mutually satisfying and truly worthwhile.

AND THE BEAT GOES ON . . .

Massachusetts law now requires the arrest of men violating restraining orders, whether they are husbands, roommates, or boyfriends. Women must be notified before the men are released from jail. During the two months before that law was passed, five women, all of whom had obtained restraining orders against their husbands, died.

One of those for whom the law came too late was Norma Starling of Foxborough. Her husband, Albert, had been ordered to stay away from her. In December, 1990, she was found dead in her bedroom.

Turners Falls is a tiny town in northern Massachusetts with a population of only 4,500. During an 18-month time span in 1989-1990, four women were murdered by their husbands. And the beat goes on.

Bibliography

Adams, David. "Identifying the Assaultive Husband in Court: You Be the Judge." *Boston Bar Journal*, Vol. 33, No. 4, p. 23, July-August, 1989.

Adams, David. "Counseling Men Who Batter: A Profeminist Analysis of Five Treatment Models," in K. Yllo and M. Bograd (eds.) *Feminist Perspective on Wife Abuse*, Sage, Beverly Hills, CA, 1988.

Adams, David. "Stages of Anti-Sexist Awareness Change for Men Who Batter," In L. Dickstein and C. Nadelson (eds.) *Family Violence*, Appi Press, Washington, DC, 1989.

Armitage, Susan and Jameson, Elizabeth, eds., *The Women's West*. University of Oklahoma Press, Norman and London, 1987.

Baden, Michael, MD and Hennessee, Judith. *Unnatural Death: Confessions of a Medical Examiner*. Ivy Books, New York, 1990.

Bean, Constance. *Methods of Childbirth, Revised Edition*. Doubleday and Co., New York, 1982.

Bean, Constance. *Methods of Childbirth: The Completely Updated Version of a Classic for Today's Woman*. William Morrow and Co., New York, 1990.

Blinder, Martin, MD. *Lovers, Killers, Husbands, Wives. A Court Psychiatrist Looks at Crimes of Passion*. St. Martins Press, New York, 1985.

Boston Globe, (quote from) "Ask The Globe," p. 32, Jan. 19, 1991.

Boston Globe, (Vaughn case) p. 29, Sept. 26, 1990.

Boston Globe, ("granny" case) p. 33, Sept. 12, 1990.

Boston Globe, (the judge's comment) p. 34, Dec. 6, 1990.

Boston Globe, (Howard case) p. 23, Jan. 28, 1990.

Boston Globe, (Telisnor case) p. 22, Feb. 2, 1990.

Boston Globe, (Gurney case) p. 23, Dec. 3, 1990.

Boston Globe, (Douglas case) p. 21, Sept. 1, 1991.

Boston Globe, (Attleborough, MA, mall murder) p. 51, Oct. 3, 1990.

Boston Globe, (Dunn case) p. 26:1, May 12, 1987.

Boston Herald, "The All-American Sociopath," p. 5, Jan. 14, 1990.

Boston Herald, (Freeman case) p. 1, October 11, 1991.

Boston Herald, (Stuart case) October 21-24, 1991.

Browne, Angela. *When Battered Women Kill*, Free Press-Macmillan, New York, 1987.

Browne, Angela and Williams, Kirk. "Exploring the Effect of Resource Availability and the Likelihood of Female-Perpetrated Homicides." *Law and Society Review*, Vol. 23, No. 1, pp. 76-94, 1989.

Bureau of Justice Statistical Special Report. "Preventing Domestic Violence Against Women," p. 1-3, Washington, DC, August, 1986.

Cape Cod Times, (Dunn case) p. 1, Mar. 5, 1991.

Cleckley, Hervey, MD. *The Mask of Sanity*. The New American Library, Mosby, NY, 1982.

Dershowitz, Alan. *Reversal of Fortune: Inside the Von Bulow Case*. Random House, New York, 1986.

Dillman, John. *Unholy Matrimony*. Macmillan, New York, 1988.

Ehrenreich, Barbara and English, Deirdre. *For Her Own Good: One Hundred Fifty Years of Expert's Advice to Women*. Anchor Press, Anchor Press/Doubleday, New York, 1989.

Englade, Ken. *Murder in Boston* (Stuart case). St. Martins Press, New York, 1990.

Fedders, Charlotte and Elliott, Laura. *Shattered Dreams*. Dell, New York, 1988.

Finn, Peter and Colson, Sarah. *Civil Protection Orders: Legislation, Current Court Practice, and Enforcement*. U.S. Department of Justice, Office of Justice Programs, March 1990.

Forward, Susan and Torres, Joan. *Men Who Hate Women and the Women Who Love Them: When Loving Hurts and You Don't Know Why*. Bantam Books, New York, 1987.

Fox, Janes and Levin, Jack. Crime, "The Boy Next Door," *Boston Magazine*, pp. 66-68, April, 1990.

Frondorf, Shirley. *Death of a Jewish American Princess: The True Story of a Victim on Trial*. Random House, New York, 1988.

Gelles, Richard and Straus, Murray. *Intimate Violence: The Definitive Study of the Causes & Consequences of Abuse in the American Family*. Simon and Schuster, New York, 1988.

Gillespie, Cynthia. *Justifiable Homicide: Battered Women, Self-Defense and the Law*. Ohio State Press, Athens, OH, 1989.

Goolkasian, Gail. *Confronting Domestic Violence: The Role of Criminal Court Judges*. National Institute of Justice/Research in Brief, U.S. Dept. of Justice, Washington, DC, p. 2, November, 1986.

Gray, Elizabeth Dodson. (ed). *Sacred Dimensions of Women's Experience*. Roundtable Press, Wellesley, MA, 1988.

Herzog, Arthur. *The Woodchipper Murder*. Henry Holt and Company, Inc., New York, 1989.

Hotaling, G. and Sugarman, D. "An Analysis of the Risk Markers in Husbands to Wife Violence: The Current State of the Knowledge." *Violence and Victims*, Vol. 1, No. 2, pp. 101-124, 1986.

Hursch, Miriam. *Women and Violence*. Van Nostrand Reinhold Co., New York, Cincinnati, Atlanta, Dallas, and San Francisco, 1981.

Illich, Ivan. *Medical Nemesis: The Expropriation of Health*. Random House, Pantheon Books, New York, 1976.

Jack, Rand and Jack, Dana C. *Moral Vision and Professional Decisions: The Changing Values of Women and Men Lawyers*. Cambridge University Press, New York, 1989.

Jones, Ann. *Women Who Kill*. Holt, Rinehart and Winston, New York, 1980.

Kahn, Sandra. *The Ex-Wife Syndrome: Cutting the Cord and Breaking Free After the Marriage Is Over*. Random House, New York, 1990.

Kleiman, Dena. *A Deadly Silence: The Ordeal of Cheryl Pierson — A Case of Incest and Murder*. The Atlantic Monthly Press, New York, 1988.

Leghorn, Lisa and Parker, Katherine. *Women's Worth: Sexual Economics and the World of Women*. Routledge and Kegan Paul, Boston, London and Hensley, 1981.

Levin, Jack. *Mass Murder: American's Growing Menace*. Berkley Books, New York, 1991.

Lyons, Albert, MD, and Petrucelli, Joseph, MD, *Medicine: An Illustrated History*. Abradale Press, Harry N. Abrams, Inc. Publishers, New York, 1987.

Maas, Peter. *In a Child's Name: The Legacy of a Mother's Murder*. Simon and Schuster, New York, 1990.

Magid, Ken and McKelvey, Carole A. *High-Risk: Children Without a Conscience*. Bantam, New York, 1989.

Marshall, Megan. *The Cost of Loving: Women and the New Fear of Intimacy*. G. P. Putnam's Sons, New York, 1984.

McCarthy, Sheryl. "Domestic Violence: A Common Tragedy." *Mount Holyoke Alumnae Quarterly*, Winter 1991, pp. 4-12, 1991.

McGill, Michael. *The McGill Report on Male Intimacy*. Holt, Rinehart and Winston, New York, 1980.

McGinniss, Joe. *Fatal Vision*. G.P. Putnam's Sons, New York, 1983.

McGinniss, Joe. *Blind Faith*. G. P. Putnam's Sons, New York, 1989.

McNulty, Faith. *The Burning Bed: The True Story of an Abused Wife*. Avon, New York, 1989. (first published by Bantam, 1981).

Middlesex News (Framingham, MA) (The Simmons case) p. 5A, August 25, 1990.

Middlesex News (National Association of Social Workers resolution) P1010A, November 15, 1990.

Middlesex News (The Robbins case) p. 35, December 5, 1990.

Middlesex News (obstetrician murder) p. 8, March 8, 1990.

Ms. "The World of Women," Vol. 1, No. 12, September-October, 1990.

Nagel, Paul C. *The Adams Women: Abigail and Louisa Adams, Their Sisters and Daughters*. Oxford University Press. Oxford, New York, 1987.

National Coalition Against Domestic Violence (see resource list) Fact Sheet, May 1988.

National Coalition Against Domestic Violence Fact Sheet, 1991.

National Institute of Justice, Fact Sheet on Domestic Violence Murders, 1990.

National Woman Abuse Prevention Project (see resource list) Fact Sheet, 1990.

Mann, Judy. "Twisted Attitudes Taint Youth." *The Washington Post*, May 6, 1988.

The New Our Bodies, Ourselves. The Boston Women's Health Book Collective Staff. Simon and Schuster, New York, 1984.

Newton, Niles. *On Birth and Women*. Birth and Life Bookstore (publishers), Seattle, WA 1990.

The New York Times, I, 14:4, (Morgan case) September 27, 1989.

The New York Times, I, p. 22, (Bianco case) March 12, 1989.

The New York Times, I, Op-Ed (article on Turners Falls murders) 24:4, I, 24:4, May 18, 1990.

The New York Times ("Preppie Murder"), II, 3:1, Aug. 9, 1990.

The New York Times (Beerle case) II, 2:5, Sept. 19, 1990.

The New York Times (Beerle case) II, 5:31, Oct. 6, 1990.

The New York Times (Guenther case) I, 19:1, Apr. 21, 1989.

NiCarthy, Ginny. *Getting Free: A Handbook for Women in Abusive Relationships*. Seal Press, Seattle, WA, 1982.

"No Way Out." *Ladies Home Journal*, Vol. CVII, No. 4, pp. 126-134, April 1990.

Norwood, Robin. *Women Who Love Too Much: When You Keep Wishing and Hoping He'll Change*. Jeremy P. Tarcher, Inc., Los Angeles, CA, Distributed by St. Martins Press, New York, 1985.

Pienciak, Richard T. *Deadly Masquerade: A True Story of High Living, Depravity, and Murder*. E. P. Dutton, New York, 1990.

Pilot's Wife. Chronicle (Regina Brown case) Channel 5, Boston (ABC), Aug. 15, 1991.

Sandiford, Kay and Burgess, Alan. *Shattered Night*. Warner Books, New York, 1984.

Sanford, Linda Tschirhart and Donovan, Mary Ellen. *Women and Self-Esteem*. Anchor Press/Doubleday, New York, 1984.

Schechter, Susan. *Women and Male Violence: The Visions and Struggles of the Battered Women's Movement*. South End Press, Boston, MA, 1982.

Scully, Diana. *Men Who Control Women's Health*. Houghton Mifflin Co., Boston, MA, 1980.

Shaevitz, Marjorie and Shaevitz, Morton. *Making It Together as a Two Career Couple*. Houghton Mifflin, Boston, MA, 1980.

Sherman, Lawrence and Berk, Richard. "The Minneapolis Domestic Violence Experiment." *Police Foundation Reports*, Police Foundation, Washington, DC 20006, (undated).

Sherman, Lawrence. Domestic Violence. *National Institute of Justice Crime File Study Guide*. U.S. Department of Justice.

Siegel, Rachel Josefowitz. "Women's Dependency in a Male-Centered Value System: Gender-Based Values Regarding Dependence and Independence." *Women and Therapy*, Vol. 7, No. 1, 1988.

Smith, Joan. *Misogynies: Reflections of Myths and Malice.* Fawcett Columbo, New York, 1990.

Solomon, Barbara. *In the Company of Educated Women: A History of Women and Higher Education in America.* Yale University Press, New Haven, CT, 1985.

Straus, Murray, Gelles, R.A. and Steinmetz, S.C. *Behind Closed Doors: Violence in America.* Doubleday, New York, 1980.

Taub, N. and Schneider, M. "Perspectives on Women's Subordination and the Role of Law" in D. Kairys (ed.) *The Politics of Law: A Progressive Critique*, Pantheon Book, New York, 1982.

Thernstrom, Melanie. *The Dead Girl.* Pfefferblit, Elaine (ed.). Pocket Books, New York, 1990.

Understanding Domestic Violence Fact Sheets, National Woman Abuse Prevention Project, 1990.

U.S.A. Today, (Ohio's imprisoned battered women) p. 1, Oct. 4, 1990.

Walker, Lenore. *The Battered Woman.* HarperCollins, New York, 1980.

Walker, Lenore. *Terrifing Love: Why Battered Women Kill and How Society Responds.* HarperCollins, NY, 1989.

Weiss, Robert. *Staying the Course: The Emotional and Social Lives of Men Who Do Well at Work.* Free Press (Div. of Macmillan) New York, 1990.

Wertz, Richard and Wertz, Dorothy. *Lying-In: A History of Childbirth in America.* Yale University Press, New Haven, CT, 1989.

"Women Under Assault." *Newsweek.* Vol. CXVL, No. 3, pp. 23-25, July 16, 1990.

Wright, William. *The Von Bulow Affair.* Delacorte Press, New York, 1983.

Wylie, Evan M. "The Night Air Raid on Boston," *Yankee Magazine*, Vol. 54, No. 5, pp. 76-81, 120-21, May, 1990.

Resources

National Criminal Justice
Department of Justice Clearinghouse
8255 H Patuxent Range Rd.
Jessup, MD 20794

U.S. Department of Justice
The National Victims Resource Center
Box 6000-AIQ
Rockville, MD 20850
800-627-6872
or 301-251-5525
or 301-251-5519

The National Woman Abuse Prevention Project
200 P St. NW
Suite 508
Washington, DC 20036
202-857-0216

National Coalition Against Domestic Violence
P.O. Box 34103
Washington, DC 20043-4103
202-638-6388

National Clearinghouse for Battered Women
125 S. 9th Street, Suite 302
Philadelphia, PA 19107
215-351-0010

Emerge, Inc.
18 Hurley St., Suite 23
Cambridge, MA 02141
617-547-9870

National Criminal Justice Reference Center
16 Research Blvd.
Rockville, MD 20880
301-251-5500

Emergency Telephone Number: 1-800-333-SAFE

Index